# POSITIVE DISCIPLINE

## FOR TEENAGERS

## Also in the Positive Discipline Series

# POSITIVE DISCIPLINE

## FOR TEENAGERS

Empowering Your Teens
and Yourself Through
Kind and Firm Parenting

*Revised 3rd Edition*

**JANE NELSEN, ED.D., AND LYNN LOTT, M.A.**

Harmony Books · NEW YORK

Published in the United States by Harmony Books, an imprint of the
Crown Publishing Group, a division of Random House LLC,
a Penguin Random House Company, New York.
www.crownpublishing.com

Harmony Books is a registered trademark, and the Circle colophon is a
trademark of Random House LLC.

Previous editions of this work were published by Prima Publishing,
Roseville, California, in 1994 and 2000, and subsequently published in
paperback by Three Rivers Press, an imprint of the Crown Publishing
Group, a division of Random House LLC, New York, in 2012.

The case studies are based on actual events, but names have been omitted or
changed to protect the privacy of the people involved.

All products mentioned in this book are trademarks of their respective
companies.

Library of Congress Cataloging-in-Publication Data is available upon
request.

ISBN 978–0–7704–3655–1
eISBN 978–0–7704–3656–8

Printed in the United States of America

Illustrations by Paula Gray
Cover photograph by Jose Luis Pelaez, Inc.

10 9 8

Third Edition

*To parents and teens,*
*to help them make the transition*
*from childhood to adulthood*
*joyful and empowering.*

# CONTENTS

# CONTENTS

# POSITIVE DISCIPLINE

## FOR TEENAGERS

# INTRODUCTION

Remember when your teen was a baby just learning to walk? What a milestone. You didn't want to miss any of it, and you were very supportive and encouraging. You would take her little hands in yours and start walking along with her—but you knew you had to let go in order for her to walk by herself. You also knew she might fall when you let go, but you had faith that this was just part of the process.

So, you let go, and she took a few wobbly steps and fell. What did you do? You probably encouraged, "Look what you did! You took a few steps. You can do it. Let's try again." You were both having a great time. When she got tired of the game and didn't want to practice walking anymore, you backed off and waited awhile. You had faith that she would master walking in time.

Meanwhile, you prepared her environment. You childproofed your home. You covered sharp corners and removed breakable objects that could hurt your child. You created a safe space in which she could expand her skills. We call this "bridge building," and you are the bridge builder. When your children are small and helpless, you build bridges that have sides close together, so your children have safety with room to move about, experiment, learn, and grow. As your children get older and more skilled, you move the "sides of their bridges" farther apart so they have more room to move about freely while continuing to be safe.

Now you have a teen who is learning to be an adult. Where are the sides of the bridge today? Are you closing them in because of your fears? Are you expanding them to support his process? Do you know you have to let go before he can master adulthood? Do you know that when you do let go, he will stumble and fall? When he falls or makes a mistake, do you understand that this is just part of the growing process? (Didn't you stumble and fall and make mistakes?) Do you encourage and cheer and show your faith in him to make it?

Adolescence is an important part of the growing-up process. During this time, teens try to find out who they are and separate from their parents. Brain research confirms this, explaining that "the adolescent brain . . . casts the teens less as a rough draft than as an exquisitely sensitive, highly adaptable creature wired almost perfectly for the job of moving from the safety of home into the complicated world outside" (http://ngm.nationalgeographic.com/2011/10/teenage-brains/dobbs-text).

The problem is that most parents use many parenting tools during this time that make situations worse instead of better, even to the point of impeding and stopping the teen brain from doing its job. This book will help you educate, challenge, and support teens in an atmosphere of mutual respect that affirms your self-worth as well as the self-worth of your children. This book will give you tools to help your teens become the highly functional adaptive adults they can be. An added bonus is that you'll learn to explore your own unresolved teen issues and move yourself forward too.

Every chapter in this book has such important information that it was difficult to decide which chapters should be at the beginning. We thought all of them warranted at least first or second status. Therefore, read the chapters in any order that appeals to you, because all of them will help you retrain yourself so you can "parent" your teen more effectively.

This book is about kind, firm, and encouraging parenting. We know that going through the teen years can be like going through a war zone for both you and your teens. Kindness and firmness can fall away and be replaced by less encouraging parenting methods. It is easy to lose your sense of awe along with your sense of humor. Remember how cute and adorable you thought your teen was when he stumbled as a baby—and now you may look at your teen and ask yourself, "What have I created? Who is this person? How did this happen? What do I do now?" Many people will tell you that control (through punishment and rewards) is just what your teen needs.

Although control sometimes provides the illusion of success on a short-term basis, children who are raised with choices, responsibility, and accountability are more likely to develop the social and life skills that will serve them well throughout their lives. This book will help you find answers and principles that work instead of throwing in the towel or giving up on your child or yourself. Working with your teenager can become an opportunity to learn or relearn the meaning of mutual respect. When you learn to parent with kindness and firmness instead of control, you'll discover what a fascinating individual your teen is.

If you have parented your children with an iron fist up to this point, your teens will love you for giving them more room. However, they may misunderstand what having more freedom and choices truly means. In that case it will be up to you to help them learn the responsibility that goes with choices. Giving up control is not about permissiveness. It is about respectfully sharing control. This book will show you many ways to get that message across successfully.

If you have spoiled and overprotected your children, your teens won't be thrilled to start taking more responsibility. They may be used to you doing everything for them. They may think that responsibility is your job. They may be unskilled and lazy and maybe even a little bit afraid. What if they really can't do what is needed? What if they look stupid trying? What if it is stressful taking on more? Be prepared when your teens try to convince you that it is your job as the parent to continue doing for them what they could learn to do for themselves. Be ready for anger at you as you hold them accountable for their behavior. Once they finish their "temper tantrums," you will be pleased at how easily they take to being more responsible, and they will like their new feelings of capability and competence.

Your job is to prepare your teens for life. Perhaps you wish you had started when they were younger. That would have been nice, but if you didn't, it is time to start now. Remember to take small steps and work on your new skills one at a time until you feel more comfortable with them. You'll find parenting so much easier when you do this. It is possible to keep the joy in parenting teens.

# HOW DO YOU KNOW WHEN YOUR CHILD BECOMES A TEEN?

## WHEN YOUR CHILD NO LONGER THINKS YOU HANG THE STARS

When Sally became a teenager, her mother thought Sally had become a different person. She dressed differently, had different friends, became a rock fan, and started playing the guitar. Underneath, she was still Sally, but now she had taken on a new role: Sally "the rocker." A friend asked Sally's mother, "When Sally was little, was she interested in superheroes? Did she ask you to sew a 'W' on her leotard so she could pretend to be Wonder Woman? Did you think it was cute?" Mom smiled as she remembered how cute she thought Sally was at this stage of her life. Her friend continued, "Could you think of her that way now? Imagine that she's put on the suit of a rocker. That's what is going on; she's trying on an identity, but the identity is not who Sally really is."

It may help to remember how different *your* personality is now from the way you were as a teen. Even though living with your adolescent child may seem to last forever, adolescence is just a brief part of the growing process. It is by no means the final destination.

## THE DREAM TEEN AND THE NORMAL TEEN

In our workshops on parenting teenagers, we challenge preconceived notions about teens through an activity called "Draw a Teen" (from the manual *Teaching Parenting the Positive Discipline Way* by Lynn Lott and Jane Nelsen, 6th edition, 2008). We form two groups. One group is asked to draw a "normal" teen—how most parents see their teens. We invite them to exaggerate. The composite teen is self-centered, listens to loud music, defies authority, prefers friends to family, has a messy room decorated with posters, values cars and an independent lifestyle, conforms to the clothing styles of peers (no matter how gross), is wearing earphones and is playing video games, smokes, and drinks alcohol. Comments from the group include:

> "Well, this is an exaggeration. All teens aren't like this."
> "But it sure does depict the rebelliousness because most of
>     them are a lot like this."
> "It helps to be reminded that my teen would not be normal if
>     he cleaned his room."
> "Come to think about it, I was like that once."

This last comment was a nice reminder to the group that we all continue to grow and change beyond adolescence.

The other group is asked to draw a "dream" teen, or how most parents think they want their teens to be. This composite teen is voted prom queen or king, keeps agreements ("I promise to be there on time, as always"), volunteers to help, loves to talk to parents ("Let me tell you everything about my life"), eats only healthy food, doesn't watch television, is very athletic, earns two scholarships (one athletic and one academic), scores high on the SATs, lines up a summer job by January, supplies his or her own money for hair or makeup and saves the rest for college and a car, respects everyone (including siblings), is respectfully assertive, doesn't waste time on video games, and is an A student. Comments from the group include:

> "A teen like this wouldn't have any friends. No one could
> stand him or her."
> "I have friends who have a teen like this and I can't stand
> her."
> "My teen is like this, although she seems pretty stressed most
> of the time."
> "I can see that I expect my teen to be perfect, even though I'm
> not."
> "I know a few teens like this and I think they're terrific."

Parents often see the dream teen as the "good kid." You may not have thought about this, but these teens may have sold out to become pleasers and approval junkies. Their parents use them as the standard and say to siblings, "Why can't you be more like your brother or sister? At least I have one that doesn't give me any trouble." The "good kid" may feel significant only if he or she is getting this kind of praise. Many teens like this fall apart when they make their first big mistake. Some cannot handle the competition when they get to college and discover they are not the only special student. Unable to handle this pressure, some even commit suicide because they don't think they can stay on top. Others start their individuation very late, sometimes wasting their freshman year in college partying instead of studying now that they are not feeling pressured by their parents.

What all teens are trying to figure out is, "Who am I, and am I good enough?" That journey can look very different from the outside, depending on the teen. Don't be fooled by appearances. It's pretty tough to go through adolescence without some insecurity. Keep in mind that if you fantasize about having a dream teen, that kid might be struggling with issues of perfectionism.

## YOUR FEELINGS LET YOU KNOW WHEN YOUR CHILD HAS BECOME A TEEN

Most dramatic changes with your kids are accompanied by a feeling response from you. Think how excited you were when your kids were potty trained. Remember how you felt when your kid said "NO" to everything you asked. Flash back to your feelings when your kids started school or had their first overnight at a friend's house. Now think about some of the feelings you've had as your kids have evolved into adolescence. Can you match the shock and/or stress experienced by the following parents?

Herb recalled the day he inadvertently discovered his eleven-year-old daughter, Kim, had sent 210 text messages in less than a day to a boy in her class. Most of the texts referred to how much they liked each other and that they wanted to kiss each other. Herb's other daughter, fifteen-year-old Macy, had no interest in boys or even texting, so it took him by surprise to realize that his eleven-year-old daughter had become a teen.

Maxine took her stepson shopping for a new winter jacket. When the sales clerk put the jacket in a shopping bag, her stepson walked away and started heading out of the store, leaving the bag on the counter. Maxine grabbed the bag, irritated that her stepson was acting so unappreciative. When she met him at the car, she asked him what was going on. He said, "I wasn't going to have anyone see me carrying a *shopping bag* through the mall. That's lame." Maxine didn't know whether she wanted to hug him or shoot him.

Sandi remembered the shock she felt when her nephew, who never noticed if his socks matched or his hair was combed, showed up in pants hanging below his waist, tennis shoes without laces, and a head full of mousse. He had mastered the latest "teen" look.

Pete told his friend, "I don't know what's going on with my thirteen-year-old son, Trevor. One minute he's my best friend and the next he's yelling at me and treating me like the enemy. I'm starting to come down hard on him so he doesn't think he can get away with that lousy behavior. I can't remember when I've felt so angry." Pete's friend couldn't help laughing. "Pete," he said, "welcome to the world of teenagers. You've been anointed."

## ANOINTMENT TO TEEN PARENTING CAN BE STRESSFUL

Stress is the space between your thoughts of how life should be and how life really is. This definition of stress (although different from what you may have heard) can be very helpful. Since stress is created by your thoughts, you can feel less stressed by becoming aware of the thoughts and looking either for ways to change how life is or what you think it should be. This method can be done without deep breathing (though it won't hurt you to take a few deep breaths) or jogging (though we encourage exercise of all kinds) or taking pills or having a drink (really). In the following activity, we'll show you how easy it can be to reduce stress.

Grab a sheet of paper. At the top of the paper, start by writing down your view of how you think it *should be* with your teen. Now write down how it *is* across the bottom of the paper. Look at the space between the top and the bottom of the paper, and in large letters that fill all the space, write the word "STRESS." Stress is represented by the space between how life should be (according to you) and how life is.

At this point you can see why you're feeling so stressed—there's probably a big gap between the two. Now think about what you do when you're stressed. Jot it down on your paper somewhere in the middle of the sheet. What you're writing down are your coping behaviors for dealing with stress. If you look closely, your coping behaviors could be increasing your stress.

Here's the tricky part. It's called "paper folding." Your job is to fold the bottom of the paper to meet the top of the paper so that both lines you wrote are now next to each other. (Parents, you may need to ask your teens to do this for you.) As you look at the two lines close together without the stress in between, what are you thinking, feeling, and deciding?

Aimee tried this activity. At the top she wrote, "It drives me crazy when my son procrastinates and waits until the last minute to get his homework done. I hate nagging him all the time."

At the bottom she wrote, "No matter what I do, he just gets angry and procrastinates more. The frustrating thing is that he usually gets his assignments done, but he creates so much stress for himself and for me."

Aimee shared that the big gap between the top of the paper and the bottom was a good representation of her stress. The way she handled the stress was to feel angry and obsess about, "Why can't he just do what he is supposed to do?" Then she interrupts whatever he is doing and bugs him to get his assignments done. She threatens him with loss of privileges and feels angry when it doesn't work. Then she thinks of herself as a failure as a mom because she can't change him.

When she folded the paper so the lines were next to each other without the big gap, she said, "What a waste. All my anger and nagging doesn't change a thing. I wonder what would happen if I just acknowledged him for pulling his homework out of the hat at the last minute? Would that just reinforce his procrastination? Well, what I'm doing isn't changing anything. I can at least give up my stress. And it would be fun to watch the look on his face when I compliment him instead of nagging him."

This stress activity has helped many parents gain awareness that eliminated (or greatly reduced) their stress. You can also reduce your stress when you understand that who your teens are today is not who they will be forever.

## WHO THEY ARE TODAY IS NOT WHO THEY WILL BE FOREVER

When Mary was a teenager, her mother constantly nagged her about leaving her dirty dishes in her room or in the sink. Now Mary nags her husband about leaving his dirty dishes around the house or in the sink. Brian seemed self-centered and selfish as a teen. As an adult he is a social worker who advocates for people in need.

Think of yourself as a teenager. In what ways are you different as an adult than you were then? Are you more responsible? Do you have more purpose and motivation in life? Are you less selfish? Are you more considerate of others? You might find it helpful to make a list of the dramatic ways you have changed since you were a teenager.

Although it may seem otherwise, teens have not grown up yet. Their behavior is only temporary. Teens want to explore how they are different from their families, how they feel and what they think about things, and what their own values are. This process of separation from the family is called "individuation."

Teenage individuation can start as early as ten or eleven and as late as eighteen or nineteen. Some people never individuate (other than changing physically), or wait until adulthood to make the big steps described in the following characteristics of individuation, which are discussed in more detail after the list.

## CHARACTERISTICS OF INDIVIDUATION

1. Adolescents have a need to find out who they are.
2. Individuation often looks like rebellion because teens are testing family values.
3. Adolescents go through huge physical and emotional changes.
4. Peer relationships take precedence over family relationships.
5. Teens explore and exercise personal power and autonomy.
6. Teens have a great need for privacy from their parents.
7. Parents become an embarrassment to their teens.
8. Teens see themselves as omnipotent and all knowing.

Keep in mind that these characteristics occur on a continuum from hardly at all to almost all the time. Teenage development can look very different from teen to teen.

## ADOLESCENTS HAVE A NEED TO FIND OUT WHO THEY ARE

You know that your children are individuating when they start keeping secrets from you. Do you remember your own teen secrets? When we ask parents to do an activity called "Teen Secrets" (What did you do as a teen that you didn't want your parents to know about?), there is a lot of laughter as they share their stories about sneaking out at night, experimenting with drugs and alcohol, sex in the backseats of cars, tipping over cows, and pranks that would warrant jail sentences today. These parents are CEOs of companies, teachers, principals, mechanics, doctors, plumbers, fathers, and mothers who are scared that their children are doing what they did as teens.

## INDIVIDUATION OFTEN LOOKS LIKE REBELLION

Although most parents worry when their teenagers rebel, it would be more appropriate to worry if they didn't. Teenagers must begin their separation from their families, and rebellion gives them the ability to do this. At first, teens may rebel by challenging what is important to their families (family values) or zeroing in on what their parents want and then doing exactly the opposite. Later, they may rebel in other ways—but at first individuation is primarily a reaction against their parents, and doing the opposite is the simplest, most natural way of being different. If teens are not allowed to rebel, they may do it in their twenties, thirties, or fifties. Teens who don't rebel (individuate) may become approval junkies—afraid to take risks or to feel comfortable with who they are.

When teens can go through their process of individuation in a supportive atmosphere (see Chapter 9), they are more likely to readopt family values in their twenties. The more they encounter disrespectful judgment, punishment, and control, the more likely they will get "stuck" in their individuation process, and the less likely it is that they will come back to family values.

## ADOLESCENTS GO THROUGH HUGE PHYSICAL AND EMOTIONAL CHANGES

Whether they like it or not, adolescents are maturing physically and sexually, undergoing biological processes that are essentially out of their control. In addition to the tumultuous, contradictory feelings these major changes cause, adolescents may feel anxiety regarding their rate of change—they may think their physical maturation is too quick or too slow in relation to that of their peers. (Most parents would prefer their children to mature slowly, but nature has its own patterns.)

The physical maturation process, with its sudden and powerful hormonal changes, causes mood swings. Without premeditation, teens are delightful one minute and biting your head off the next. In addition, some teens are in such a rapid rate of physical growth that they experience real "growing pains," where their bodies actually hurt.

During adolescence, most researchers believe the brain goes through a "second wave" of development. Puberty begins, too, and the combination of hormones and new brain growth can be overwhelming. The prefrontal cortex, which is responsible for many "adult" functions such as impulse control, emotional management and regulation, and problem solving, is still maturing. Teens process emotions and make decisions primarily through the limbic system (the so-called primitive brain). In other words, they react to others, identify their own feelings, and make decisions with their "gut instinct." This is part of the reason why teens can be impulsive, dramatic, and liable to take risks. They need help identifying their feelings and then connecting with their heads to think things through (covered more thoroughly in Chapter 6 on communication skills).

Brain development does not excuse poor choices and behavior, but it does help parents and teachers understand why teens need connection, kind and firm discipline that teaches, and good life skills. (And patience—lots of patience!) Understanding brain development can also help adults take teens' behavior less personally, remaining calm, kind, and firm as they set boundaries and follow through.

## PEER RELATIONSHIPS TAKE PRECEDENCE OVER FAMILY RELATIONSHIPS

This may drive you crazy, but one of the biggest teen indicators is when your kids start worrying whether they are "in" or "out" of cool crowds and the decisions they make about themselves based on their status. They may decide they are "winners" or "losers" and then compound their "rebellion" behavior if they believe they are a "loser." It can become very confusing and very traumatic. How can they possibly spare time to worry about their family relationships—when deep down they are worried about feeling safe in their place of belonging with their peers?

Although peer relationships help teens in their task of separation, parents often interpret their preoccupation with friends as rejection or rebellion. Don't take their individuation process personally. Have patience. If you avoid power struggles and criticism, your teen will become one of your best friends in his or her twenties.

## TEENS EXPLORE AND EXERCISE PERSONAL POWER AND AUTONOMY

Have you felt shocked when a friend or neighbor told you how nice and polite your teen is? Did you wonder, "Who are you talking about?"

This can be a sign of good parenting. Your teen feels safe to "test" his or her power around you, but practices what he or she is learning from you while out in public.

Teens have a strong desire to find out what they are capable of—they need to test their power and importance in the world. This means that they want to decide what they can do for themselves without being directed and ordered. Parents often take this as a challenge to their own power, thus creating power struggles. The key is learning to support teen exploration in respectful ways that teach important life skills. The safer teens feel at home, the less traumatic their individuation process.

## TEENS HAVE A GREAT NEED FOR PRIVACY

You may wonder why your teenager needs privacy from you when he or she seems to broadcast every thought and feeling to the whole world via Facebook or other social network sites. Could it be that teens aren't necessarily rational? Perhaps you could simply quit asking questions and become a friend on their Facebook pages.

Because their rate of development moves so fast and is out of their control, teens can be embarrassed to have their families watching them. As teens try to figure out what's important to them, they may engage in activities without parental approval before deciding for themselves that they might not want to do the activities after all. To escape getting in trouble or to avoid disappointing you, teens will figure out how to test activities that you may not approve of without your knowledge, like hiding clothes and makeup in their backpack and changing at school, sneaking cigarettes, checking out the R-rated movies you have told them they can't see, writing their most private thoughts in a journal, or hanging out with kids they think you wouldn't approve of. Another way teens protect their privacy is by overt lying.

Teens often lie because they love you and they want to protect you. They want to be able to do what they do without hurting your feelings. Other times, they lie to protect themselves—from your harsh opinions and possibly harsh actions. Here's what teens say about lying:

> "I lie to go to parties because my mom won't even negotiate
> with me if there aren't some parents there."
> "I'm pretty honest with my mom because she treats me

like I'm older than I am, and she teaches me how to be a responsible drinker."

"I lied when I was a freshman and sophomore. Then I decided I didn't want to lie to them. I told them, 'cuz I don't want to lie, and now I tell them everything. I've been through lots with my mom."

"I don't share things they wouldn't want to hear. They only want to hear good stuff, so I make up things, like, 'There was this girl at the party who was so retarded who got drunk.' (The girl is really me.)"

"I would feel lower about myself if I told the truth because my mother wouldn't understand, because of how she was raised."

"Telling the truth depends on your parents: some you can tell and others would chain us to our beds."

When you understand your teen's motivation for lying, you can be much more effective in creating an atmosphere where your teen feels safe to tell you the truth—most of the time. How many of you would tell the truth if you knew you would receive blame, shame, or pain? How many of you would tell the truth if that would mean you couldn't do something you really wanted to do?

It is unlikely that you would tell the truth to make sure your parents would protect you from learning from your own mistakes. On the other hand, you might tell the truth if your parents had faith in you to make your own mistakes while helping you explore possibilities. Chances are greater that you would tell the truth if you knew that your parents would be supportive and encouraging even if you made mistakes.

Your teen's need for privacy can be very scary for you. You may worry that you are not being a responsible parent if you don't know everything your teen is doing. You may fear that your teen might do drugs (or engage in some other disastrous activity) if you are not vigilant. We have news for you: if teens are going to engage in these activities, they will do it in spite of parents' vigilance. They will just go underground so they have less chance of getting caught.

The best prevention for possible disaster is to build kind and firm relationships with your teens—let them know that they are unconditionally important to you. Keep your eyes open and be ready to lend a hand when your teen needs your adult wisdom and help to figure out what is important to him or her.

## PARENTS BECOME AN EMBARRASSMENT TO THEIR TEENS

Sometimes teens act embarrassed around their parents and families in public or may even refuse to be seen with them. The affection that may have been a normal part of family life may suddenly become taboo. They may even put down their parents and let them know how stupid they think they are. This is a temporary condition, unless you make an issue of it that builds resentment for the future.

Usually, the way kids act around their parents does not represent how they really feel. When we work with teens, we often ask them for four or five adjectives to describe their parents. Their choices are usually incredibly encouraging. Parents who have been convinced that their teens hate them hear themselves described as nice, friendly, helpful, and fair, even though their teens have been fighting with them morning, noon, and night. One stepparent, upon hearing her stepson list her as part of the family, said, "Oops, I don't think you're supposed to put me in." He said, "Why not? You're part of the family." Although she thought of him that way, she had no idea he felt the same about her.

## TEENS SEE THEMSELVES AS OMNIPOTENT AND ALL KNOWING

Parents who try to tell teens how to dress or eat or what they can or can't do just don't seem to understand that teens never get sick, don't get cold, don't need sleep, and can live forever on junk food or no food at all. Many parents wonder how their children even survive these years, but the facts are that most teens do. To some it may seem that the methods we advocate are permissive and increase the chances of drastic consequences. The opposite is true.

### Not Permissiveness

Sometimes we get a strong reaction from parents who read the list of characteristics of individuation. Their comments are very similar, "You can't just stop being a parent and let kids go off on their own to individuate." That last word is said with a great deal of sarcasm.

We do not advocate letting kids go off on their own. This would be permissiveness—a kind of parenting that deprives young people of parental support while learning valuable lessons. Teens need guidance, but not external controls, which only increase rebellion.

## DON'T FAN THE FLAMES OF REBELLION

Keep in mind that teenage rebellion is usually temporary (one to five years). However, if you do not understand that rebellion is part of individuation and you instead make it an issue, the rebellion may extend into adulthood. When parents are using kind and firm methods, rebellion is less likely to be extreme. Individuation often becomes all-out rebellion when you invalidate the normal growth process.

If you could simply relax and remember that these are the years when your children are experimenting in an attempt to find out what they think, you could enjoy them more. If you could relax, you could trust that who they are now is in no way a reflection on you or indicative of who they will be when they grow up. With these new attitudes, you could focus on long-term parenting and learn to be a guide and facilitator your teens could trust.

## KIND AND FIRM PARENTING TOOLS TO REMEMBER

1. If you are arguing, scolding, lecturing, and shaming with no success, you might have a child who has just become a teen. Put on your "Isn't this interesting?" hat and sit back to watch for the signs.

2. Find out what your teen's issues are instead of assuming they are the same as the ones you had when you were a teen. Times change.

3. Remind yourself that your teen is growing up, not a grown-up.

4. Look at what you might be doing to feed the flames of rebellion instead of honoring the individuation process. Review the characteristics of individuation.

5. Make an effort to get into your teen's world and honor the individuality of your teen's trip through adolescence.

6. Balance your teen's need for privacy with special individual time and with kind and firm support.

7. Practice the tips for "growing" teens instead of resorting to punishment and control.

### *Practical Application Activity*

We suggest that your relationship with your teenager is valuable enough to spend a short amount of time each week writing in a journal the answers to the activity following each chapter. Doing so will help you increase your awareness or practice a new behavior. You may feel encouraged by discovering how much innate wisdom you have, given a little guidance in the right direction. By taking time to write your answers in a journal, you will more easily gain insights, learn from your mistakes, expand your perspective, and tap into that innate wisdom of yours.

When you realize that the things your teens do and say are statements about them and not about you, you can stop blaming yourself for their behavior or taking it personally. Your children are separate people from you, and the mistakes and successes they make are theirs to learn from and to own.

1. To help you realize that your children are separate from you, pick one of their behaviors that really bugs you or choose from the following list:
   a. Cutting classes
   b. Spending time in room
   c. Refusing to go on family vacation
   d. Trading outfits you gave as gifts
   e. Moodiness
   f. Forgetting to do chores
   g. Not wanting to sit with you at a movie theater
   h. Not wanting to go to college
2. Read the following two attitudes:
   a. Taking it personally means I tell myself that my child's behavior has something to do with my failures or successes. For example, I'm a terrible parent; I'm a good parent; What will others think?; How could he do this after all I have done for him?; She must hate me, or she wouldn't behave this way.
   b. Not taking it personally means I tell myself that my child's behavior has to do with him or her, not me. For example, This is important to him; She needs to find out for herself; He is exploring what life and values mean to him; This is not important to her; I have faith that he can learn whatever he needs to learn from his mistakes and challenges; I wonder what this means to her.
3. Return to the behavior that bugs you and write out how you would act with attitude A. Then write how you would act with attitude B.
4. Talk with your teen about what you have learned by doing this activity.

# 2

# WHOSE SIDE ARE YOU ON?

## MAKING SURE THE MESSAGE OF LOVE
## GETS THROUGH

Teens today want to be pilots of their own life planes. They want their parents to love them, support them, and accept them but leave them alone to pursue their lives—except when they want something. Sometimes teens act as if they want to kick their parents off their planes.

Many parents want to pilot their teens' life planes. They are scared that if they turn over the controls to their teens, they will get into trouble, get hurt, or fail—maybe even die. With this fear in mind, they often become ineffective parents and invite more rebellion with their overcontrolling ways.

You can remain on the life plane of your teenager as a copilot if you learn the Positive Discipline skills of a kind and firm parent—being available for support and guidance when necessary while encouraging your teen to be a skilled and responsible pilot. And like any copilot, there may be moments when you get to fly the plane, but they are rare.

Connie wanted to learn how to be a skilled copilot in her son Brad's life so she joined a parent study group to learn more about Positive Discipline. In this group she soon discovered why her efforts to pilot her son's plane were failing miserably. Through experiential activities she was able to "get into her son's world" and experience why he rebelled when she was controlling (too firm) and why he took advantage when she flipped to the other extreme and was permissive (too kind). Once she understood the importance of being both kind and firm at the same time, Connie could hardly wait to practice what she had learned.

However, when Connie learned that Brad had been skipping school, she forgot all her new resolutions, tried to jump back into the pilot's seat, and began using her old controlling style. She cornered Brad in his room and lectured him about his irresponsible behavior.

Brad responded by telling his mom to get off his back, which hooked Connie into escalating her lecture into a heated scolding about Brad's disrespect for his elders.

Brad retorted, "I don't see you being respectful to me."

Connie was now so angry, she felt like hitting her son for speaking to her that way. Instead, flashing back to her parenting group about *making sure the message of love gets through*, she realized what was happening and changed her approach. "Son, do you know I'm on your side?"

Brad retorted, "How would I know that?" Then, with tears stinging his eyes, he said, "How can I think you're on my side when you're always putting me down?"

Connie was shocked. She honestly did not think she has been putting him down. She thought she had been pointing out his mistakes and was trying to motivate him to do better.

Connie put her arm around her son and, fighting tears of her own, said, "I had no idea I was hurting you instead of helping you. I'm so sorry."

How could Brad know that his mom was on his side when he was being bombarded with lectures and scolded about his deficiencies? Fortunately, Connie had learned enough to catch herself behaving ineffectively and was able to change her approach. As she left her son's room, she said, "Why don't we talk about this later when we're both in a better mood?"

## OLD HABITS ARE HARD TO CHANGE

Of course, as a parent, you are on your children's side, but often they won't perceive you as being on their side. In fact, too often your behavior could fool any astute observer. In the name of their children's best interests, many parents lose sight of what being on their side means and what will really help their teens develop the character and life skills they need to be successful in life.

The more anxious you are, the less your kids perceive you being on their side. Some teens wonder why you are so hard on them, seemingly all of a sudden. Perhaps as you are bombarded with frightening news about the economy and the job market, and are told over and over that more twentysomething kids are living at home while they struggle to find any job, you figure you better clamp down now. This clamping down can look like fighting over spots in coveted preschools for your younger children all the way up to crushing levels of test prep and résumé padding in preparation for college. When the media message portrays "the world has changed from when you were young, things are much harder," it becomes *very* easy to discount your own experiences (i.e., "I made mistakes, and I still turned out okay") and buy into the illusion that "if my children make mistakes, they will *not* turn out okay."

Positive Discipline is *not* about pretending the world is an easy place, nor is it a rejection of your natural desire to ensure your child is prepared to lead a happy and successful life. Positive Discipline parenting methods are specifically designed to help teens become adults who can effectively cope with those kinds of challenges and still be happy.

It can be tempting for parents, when they hear dire economic warnings, to think that their teens will be better served by straight A's (even if parents have to punish and cajole them into studying, or write their papers for them) or a spotless record (even if it means keeping them under lock and key, or lying to give them an alibi) than by being allowed to grow at their own pace and make their own mistakes. But this is a shortsighted viewpoint. The opportunities afforded straight-A students will mean nothing if they haven't learned for themselves how to pursue what is meaningful and fulfilling to them in a responsible way—learning from their mistakes.

It is easy to forget whose side you are on when you allow your fears, judgments, and expectations to take over. It's only natural at those times to return to whatever parenting style has become the most familiar. (See Chapter 3 on parenting styles for detailed information about the parenting styles that are mentioned briefly in this chapter.)

When controlling parents criticize, scold, lecture, correct, demand, use put-downs, and express their disappointment, young people do not feel supported or loved. Teens experience their controlling parents' love as conditional. They believe that the only way their parents will be "on their side" is when they do exactly what their parents want. This creates an existential crisis. How can they do what their parents want *and* discover who they want to be? (Normal rebellion is not against parents but for themselves—unless parents get too controlling.)

Permissive, spoiling parents, on the other hand, may allow their teens too much freedom without requiring responsibility. They may indulge their teens, buying them cars, electronics, and too many clothes without any contribution from their kids. Permissive parents constantly intervene to save their children from the consequences of their behavior and bail them out of situations that could be useful learning opportunities. This is not a healthy way to be on a teen's side, and it does not help kids learn the life skills they need to develop a sense of personal capability.

Nor do children feel parents are on their side if they are neglected. Neglect takes many forms, from drug addiction to workaholism to giving up because parenting is too hard or too inconvenient.

We offer seven easy tips for convincing your teens that you are for them and not against them by "connecting before correcting." If you feel your relationship regressing to old patterns, review these seven tips and try again.

## SEVEN TIPS FOR CREATING A CONNECTION WITH YOUR TEEN

1. Get into your teen's shoes and empathize.
2. Listen and be curious.
3. Stop worrying about what others think—do what is best for your teen.
4. Replace humiliation with encouragement.
5. Make sure the message of love gets through.
6. Involve your teen in focusing on solutions.
7. Make respectful agreements.

## GET INTO YOUR TEEN'S SHOES AND EMPATHIZE

You get a call from the school saying your teen has cut two classes today and has gotten a detention. Your blood starts to boil. You can't wait until your child comes home so you can let her know how angry you are and how unacceptable her behavior is. Your teen, completely unperturbed by the events at school, decides to stay after school to hang out with friends and arrives home late for dinner. As she walks in the door, you start yelling from the kitchen, "You are in so much trouble. Get in here this minute. Where have you been? What has gotten into you?"

Imagine yourself in the shoes of your teenager. How would you feel if you were treated the way you just treated her? Would you feel inspired and encouraged to do better? Would you feel confident about your capabilities to explore the world and to decide for yourself (sometimes through mistakes) what makes sense to you? Would you believe your parent is giving you the guidance and character training you need in ways that are encouraging instead of discouraging? Would you believe that your parent was "for you" or "against you"?

We hope that when you are in a situation like this, you will set aside your tirade and first make a connection with your teen. Take a deep breath and remember your bottom line—how much you love this child. Using a kind tone of voice, find out what is going on for her.

Remember Connie and Brad? Connie was caught up in the familiar trap of lecturing before listening. When she became aware that she was acting as though she were against her son instead of making a connection, Connie's first step was to find a way to get into his shoes through curiosity questions and by empathizing. She approached Brad in a spirit of support rather than aggression. She asked if Brad would like to drop out of school, as at seventeen years old he didn't legally have to attend. Suspicious of this new approach, Brad asked, "And do what?"

Connie was honest. "That's a good question. I don't know. Maybe just do what you're doing—sleep in, work in the afternoon, spend time with your friends in the evening. Of course you would have to get a job and pay rent."

For the first time in a long while, Brad dropped his defensiveness and seemed willing to share his thoughts with his mom. "I don't really want to drop out, but I would like to go to a continuation school."

Connie wondered out loud, "Why?"

Brad could sense that his mother really wanted to know, so he explained that he didn't want to be a high school dropout. In continuation school, he could take the classes he'd failed in his regular school. If he remained where he was, he'd have to take those courses during the summer, and he didn't want to ruin his summer. In addition, since continuation school allows students to progress at their own speed, Brad felt that he could do much better than simply catch up.

## LISTEN AND BE CURIOUS

Curiosity questions and careful listening show that you are on your teen's side, which then allows you to have a positive influence with your teens. (Connection before correction.) Think of a time when you didn't listen or show any curiosity. What kind of results did you get? Now, imagine that situation, and picture yourself listening and being curious without trying to fix the problem.

Being curious is different from the usual twenty questions that most parents ask. The purpose of curiosity questions is to help teens process their thinking and the consequences of their choices rather than to bring them around to your way of thinking. Don't ask questions unless you really are curious about your teen's point of view. If your teen gets punished after giving honest information, curiosity won't work.

Helping teens explore the consequences of their choices is much different from imposing consequences on them. Imposing a consequence (a poorly disguised punishment) is designed to make kids *pay for what they did* and usually invites rebellion. Curiosity questions invite kids to explore what happened, what caused it to happen, how they feel about it, and what they can *learn from their experience.*

## STOP WORRYING ABOUT WHAT OTHERS WILL THINK—DO WHAT IS BEST FOR YOUR TEEN

Once committed to being on Brad's side and supporting his idea, Connie decided to suspend her fears about what other people might think. She also put aside her stereotype of teens who go to continuation schools as losers who can't make it in regular schools. Instead, she looked at the benefits. She told Brad that she believed he would do extremely well when allowed to progress at his own speed in an atmosphere of mutual respect. (Many continuation school staffs treat teens more respectfully than regular school staffs.) Connie agreed to call both schools to find out what could be done about a transfer. In her next study group, Connie learned that it would have been even more effective to make the calls with Brad rather than for him, but she was making huge progress in her efforts to become a kind and firm parent.

Later, Connie told her parent study group,

> *I have no idea how this will turn out. I know I felt closer to my son, because I got into his world and supported him in living his life as he sees it. I got out of the power struggle that was making us both feel like losers, so we could look for solutions that would make us both feel like winners.*
>
> *I took a look at my own issues about being a "good" parent. Whenever I try to make him do what I think is best, I become a lecturing, moralizing, controlling mom—and he rebels. But when I try to support Brad in being who he is through kind and firm parenting, he's willing to talk to me and look for solutions. Whenever I worry about what others think (usually people whose opinion I don't really respect anyway), I create distance from my son. It is so rewarding to remember whose side I'm on and to act accordingly.*

A year later, Connie shared that Brad did very well in his continuation school classes. He got caught up and went back to regular classes the following year. Connie believes the reason he did well is that the solution was his idea, not a punishment. He was also able to stop rebelling *against* Connie's control and focus on actions *for* himself.

The more you change yourself instead of trying to change your teen, the more you invite your teen to be responsible, capable, and caring. Clearly, Brad cared about his education, but his solution was different from what his mother might have recommended.

Remind yourself of what is best for your child long term. Determine how you can shift your focus to what is in the best interest of your teen, instead of worrying about the judgments of others.

## REPLACE HUMILIATION WITH ENCOURAGEMENT

Connie had learned the difference between supporting her son and thwarting him. She learned that humiliating Brad did not encourage him or motivate him to do better.

A group of high school girls gave the following suggestions to adults who wanted to replace humiliation with encouragement in order to invite connection and cooperation with their teens. Review the list and share it with your teen. Ask what he or she would add to or subtract from the list:

> "Sometimes I hate talking to my parents because they make everything into a big deal. Some things are little, and we don't need to talk about them forever."
>
> "Friendly is better. It's okay for you to teach us stuff, but be more like a big sister or brother or a friend."
>
> "Never accuse us of doing something; ask instead."
>
> "If we do something wrong, don't yell, because our first response is to rebel when we are yelled at. Yelling or trying to scare us doesn't work. You sound stupid and it makes us mad. Instead, really talk to us and be honest."

## MAKE SURE THE MESSAGE OF LOVE GETS THROUGH

Lorna, a mother from Connie's parent study group, shared her success with making sure the message of love gets through. Lorna's daughter, Mara, did not come home one night. Although Lorna was both angry and afraid that Mara might be involved in drugs, she remembered from her parenting group that parents create distance by scolding and lecturing. Instead of focusing on her fear and anger, she decided to focus on making a connection.

When Mara came home the next morning, Lorna said, "I'm glad you're okay. I was worried about you. Before you say anything, I want you to know that I love you, and I'm on your side."

Mara seemed genuinely apologetic and said, "I'm really sorry, Mom. I was watching television at Stephie's and fell asleep."

Lorna said, "I can see how that could happen, but I would have appreciated a call as soon as you woke up—even if it was in the middle of the night, so I would have known you were okay." Mara gave her a hug and repeated, "I'm sorry, Mom."

Enjoying the closeness she felt with her daughter and feeling more comfortable with her new skills, she continued, "I can see that you might not want to call after you've made a mistake if you think I'm going to scold you like I usually do. I want you to know I'm going to try not to do that anymore. No matter how many times you make a mistake, you can still call me, and I'll be on your side, not against you."

Some of the other members of the class were suspicious of Mara's story and started "yes, butting": "But you let her get away with staying out all night." "But do you believe she really just fell asleep?" Lorna was not fazed because she deeply understood the concept of making sure the message of love gets through to change her relationship with her daughter. She told her classmates, "Mara had already 'gotten' away with it. She had stayed out all night. Punishing her wouldn't change that. I used to think that punishment might scare her into not doing it again. Instead, she just got better at trying to hide what she did. I also suspected that falling asleep may not have been the truth—or at least not the whole truth. The third degree about that wouldn't help or change anything. I truly believe things will change when she knows I love her, have faith in her, and when I create an environment where it is safe for her to think for herself instead of for or against me. I think it will take time to change the patterns I helped create when I parented from my fear instead of from my love, but that is what I'm going to do. Besides, after I established the foundation of love, I was able to talk with Mara, share my feelings, and work on an agreement that felt respectful to both of us."

## INVOLVE YOUR TEEN IN FOCUSING ON SOLUTIONS

Lorna could see that she had now created enough closeness to work with Mara on a solution. In the past, she would have told her what to do and threatened her with some punishment or loss of privilege if she didn't comply. Instead, replacing demands with solutions, she asked, "Could we work on an agreement about you calling me if you're going to be late?"

Mara said, "What if it's really late and you're asleep?"

Lorna said, "Even if I'm asleep, I'm not sleeping well when I don't know if you're okay. You can call me anytime."

Mara replied, "I hadn't thought about you worrying about me. I always just thought about you being mad at me. You don't need to worry about me, Mom, but I will call you whenever I'm going to be late."

That night when she got home, Mara went to her parents' bedroom and hugged them goodnight—something she hadn't done in months.

Later, Lorna told her parenting group, "What a difference! Before, I never thought how Mara would feel about my anger with her whenever she was inconsiderate. I'd just yell and accuse her. This time, I let her see how much I love her, and we were able to find a solution that worked for both of us. I still don't know if she was telling the truth about falling asleep on her friend's couch—but the way I used to act didn't encourage the truth at all. It created a big chasm in our relationship instead. This feels so much better to me. Mara's independence still scares me, but at least we have a connection that is more likely to encourage the communication I want."

The other members of the group were very touched by Lorna's wisdom and conviction. It forced them to look at their own fear-based behavior—and the unsatisfactory results they were getting.

Think of a time when you were really worried or scared about your children. Did you lecture and scold your teens instead of letting them know how much you love them and how worried you were? Did you create a connection before correction?

Most teens really don't like upsetting their parents. If you calmly say how you feel, they will hear you, even if it seems like they couldn't care less at the moment. Watch for changes in your teen's behavior in the next twenty-four hours. Usually you don't have to wait that long to see an act of kindness or friendship on his or her part. Connection often leads to self-correction.

Many parents share the "yes, but" concerns of Lorna's parenting group and believe that what Lorna did was too permissive, that her approach let Mara "get away" with disrespectful behavior, and that Lorna should have found out if Mara was lying or doing drugs. When we examine these concerns more carefully, we can see that any other approach would not solve anything; it would only make matters worse. If Mara's mom became a controlling parent, Mara would only get more rebellious and secretive. Lorna couldn't force Mara to tell the truth, but she could create an environment in which Mara feels safe to tell the truth. By being kind and firm, Mara's mom modeled respect. Lorna was wise enough to create a connection before engaging Mara in the process of working together on a solution—one that Mara would be more likely to follow because of the respectful manner in which she was involved.

## MAKE RESPECTFUL AGREEMENTS

Some parents say to their teens in a menacing tone of voice, "This is what we are going to do. Do you agree?" The teens resentfully respond, "Sure," while thinking, *Get off my back*. They may even have their fingers crossed, but they have no intention of keeping the agreement. They may simply be counting the days, hours, and minutes until they can get away and do what they want.

The agreements we encourage are ones in which you practice respectful involvement by saying to your teen, "I can't agree with that, but I'm willing to keep brainstorming until we can make an agreement that feels respectful to both of us." It's often necessary to say to a teen, "I prefer to continue this discussion until we figure something out we both like. But if that isn't possible, for now, we'll stick with things the way they are until we can make a respectful agreement."

If you make an agreement, try it out for a short time to see if the situation improves. If not, make an appointment with your teen and brainstorm some more.

## CHANGE REQUIRES PRACTICE

It takes time to change old habits. Even when you decide you want to be the copilot instead of the pilot, and even when you want to be on your teen's side, you will most likely find yourself slipping into old habits based on old fears. Making changes may feel as awkward as the wobbly experience you had when first learning to ride a bike. Keep practicing. You'll get it.

And remember that you are an important person, too. We find that parents think they should give up their needs and their lives until the kids are gone. If you parent that way, your teens will probably think the world revolves around them, even more than they already do. When you respect yourself and show your teen that you have needs and wants and a life to live, your teen will thrive.

### KIND AND FIRM PARENTING TOOLS TO REMEMBER

1. Move over to the copilot's seat so you can have a positive influence on your teens without trying to run their lives.
2. Remember that making changes takes time and you will probably slip back to your familiar parenting style when you are scared. Keep practicing.
3. Use the "Seven Tips for Creating a Connection with Your Teen" (page 25) to create a base of love and respect.
4. Ask your teen what advice he or she would give about any ways you may inadvertently be using humiliation instead of respectful communications.
5. Remember to talk with your teens first before making decisions about their lives or taking actions that will affect them.

6. When you find yourself doing the "mischief shuffle" (see information on this in Chapter 14), decide if you'd like to try a new dance that would help you be more on your own side.

7. Whenever you practice, you get better, so practice, practice, practice.

### Practical Application Activity

When your teen thinks you are on his or her side, the impulse to act out in extreme ways is greatly reduced. This activity can help you be aware of ways you are not on your teen's side and how to remedy that.

1. Recall a situation in which you treated your teen disrespectfully. In your journal, describe the situation.

2. Imagine that you are a teenager. What would it be like to have a parent who acts like you in the situation? How would you feel? What would you decide? Would you think your parent was on your side?

3. What can you learn from this activity? What could you do differently as the parent in that situation? Imagine how the situation would occur, and describe it in your journal.

4. Ask your teen whose side he or she thinks you're on. Using the seven tips for turning around your relationship, choose what you could do differently so your teen would know you were on his or her side.

# 3

# WHAT IS YOUR
# PARENTING STYLE?

## A BRICK, A RUG, A GHOST, OR A PD PARENT

Parenting styles can be encouraging or discouraging. In this chapter we discuss four parenting styles, three that are discouraging (short-term parenting) and one that is encouraging for both teens and parents (long-term parenting). Any parenting style that does not empower teens to become capable adults is short-term parenting. Successful long-term parenting, however, empowers children with the life skills they need for success—to become happy, contributing members of society.

In his chapter "On Children" in *The Prophet*, Kahlil Gibran beautifully illustrates the foundation for the parenting style we advocate:

*Your children are not your children.*
*They are the sons and daughters of Life's longing for itself.*

*They come through you, but not from you.*
*And though they are with you, yet they belong not to you.*
*You may give them your love but not your thoughts,*
*For they have their own thoughts.*
*You may house their bodies, but not their souls,*
*For their souls dwell in the house of tomorrow, which you cannot*
*visit, not even in your dreams.*
*You may strive to be like them, but seek not to make them like you.*
*For life goes not backward nor tarries with yesterday.*

Although the beauty and simplicity of Gibran's poem are inspiring, most parents do not know how to apply this poem to their own lives. As you read this book, you will acquire many ideas about how to change your parenting style and be a very active, supportive parent who is neither permissive nor controlling. We include many long-term parenting skills for dealing with challenges that concern most parents of teens—all based on respect—respect for teenagers and for parents.

## THE COMMON METHODS OF PARENTING TEENS

The first parenting style is called "control." Think of a brick. It's rigid, heavy, limited in space, has rough edges, and can be sharp and cutting. The brick symbolizes the control style of parenting. Many parents think it's their responsibility—part of their jobs as parents—to control their teenagers. Parents seem to believe that if they don't make their teens do things *for their own good*, then they are being permissive parents. These parents use some form of punishment or rewards as their primary method of control. With teenagers, the most common punishments are grounding, withdrawing privileges, taking away allowances, using physical and emotional abuse, and withdrawing love and approval.

Trying to gain control makes parents feel that they have done their job. However, controlling parents do not consider the long-term results of their methods. This kind of parenting invites children:

1. To think might makes right.
2. To believe, "I have to give up myself to be loved by you."
3. To avoid contribution unless there are external rewards.
4. To manipulate for bigger rewards.
5. To rebel or comply.

Short-term parenting can be exhausting. In this style of parenting, the parents' responsibility is to *catch* their children being *bad* so they can dish out the punishments and lectures. It is also the parents' responsibility to *catch* their children being *good* to dish out the rewards. What responsibilities are teens learning? Perhaps the only responsibility of a teen is not to get caught, to manipulate for bigger rewards, or to refuse compliance when the reward no longer matters.

If all power is taken away from teenagers, they will never have the opportunity to learn responsibility—or to make their own mistakes and learn from them. In addition, these teens will never have the opportunity to discover and set their own limits. How can teens learn to be responsible if parents continue to take that role? One of the best ways to teach children to be irresponsible is to be a controlling parent.

Example: A parent attending one of our workshops challenged us on the issue of giving up control. He explained that his fifteen-year-old daughter habitually came home later than the curfew he had set for her. The last time she came home an hour late, he grounded her for a week. When he was asked what he thought she learned from this, he said, "She learned that she can't get away with this behavior." When asked how he felt about this, he said, "I feel good. It's not my job to be her buddy. It's my job to be her parent."

Further exploration revealed that even though he had hated it when his parents grounded him as a teen, he now believed as a parent that it was his job to set rules and restrictions and to punish children when they disobeyed. He felt a sense of accomplishment that he had done his job, although he admitted that grounding did not solve the problem. His daughter continued to come home late, and he continued to ground her. He said, "Come to think of it, I acted like my daughter and continued to defy my father as long as I lived at home. I didn't keep curfew until I left home and felt like getting home early so I could get a good night's sleep. And I still don't want to have anything to do with my father. I don't want that kind of relationship with my daughter. Okay. I'm ready to learn alternatives."

We know many parents won't want to hear this, but any form of control or punishment is very disrespectful to teenagers and extremely ineffective for the goals of long-term parenting. It is sometimes appropriate to withdraw privileges from children under twelve or thirteen when the withdrawal relates to the misbehavior, is respectfully enforced, and seems reasonable, by advance agreement, to both parent and child. However, by the time children reach adolescence and see themselves as adults, they won't see grounding or removal of privileges as respectful or reasonable.

Another danger of the controlling parenting style is permanent apron strings. Children who never escape the control of their parents may decide that their whole lives revolve around doing what they think their mother

or father would want. They often grow up to become *approval junkies* who find other people to continue the job of controlling them. This can be devastating to marriages, parenting, friendships, and jobs.

Some children who were raised in a controlling environment become late bloomers. Eventually they may get into therapy, where they find support in learning to grow—support their parents didn't offer. They didn't learn the skills needed to make their own choices and decisions. It takes a while to convince late bloomers that it's okay to be separate people from their parents and to give up their mistaken perceptions of what they need to do to get approval in life.

## PERMISSIVE/OVERPROTECTIVE/RESCUING PARENTING

If you're not a brick, are you more like a rug, letting everyone walk all over you, covering up issues rather than dealing with them? Permissive parents can liken themselves to rugs, the second short-term parenting style, as they overprotect, spoil, and rescue their teens.

This kind of parent invites children to:

1. Expect undue service from others.
2. Equate love with getting others to take care of me.
3. Care more about things than about people.
4. Learn, "I can't handle being upset or feeling disappointment."
5. Believe, "I'm not capable."

The permissive style of parenting seems to make parents feel that they've done their job because they protect or rescue their children from pain or suffering. However, short-term parenting robs teenagers of learning the life skills of self-reliance and resiliency. Instead of learning that they can survive pain and disappointment, and even learn from it, children grow up extremely self-centered, convinced that the world and their parents owe them something and that they are entitled to whatever they want. Thus, permissiveness is not a good parenting style for helping teenagers become adults with good character and life skills.

Example: Coretta was a permissive parent who gave in every time her daughter, Jesse, wanted a toy or candy in the store. After all, Coretta wanted to protect Jesse from any suffering. When Jesse was late with a school assignment, Coretta was quick to rescue her by dropping all her own plans and rushing to the library or the store to get whatever was required so she could help Jesse complete the assignment.

By the time Jesse reached the eighth grade, Coretta and Jesse had a well-established process. Jesse decided that her popularity depended on being the best-dressed girl in her school. She demanded more and more clothes. If her mother said no, Jesse would plead with tears in her eyes and would threaten to quit school if she didn't get what she wanted. Coretta would give in. Imagine the kind of character and skills Jesse was developing.

When Jesse went to college, she continued her materialistic lifestyle by using credit cards. It wasn't long before she was far in debt. In desperation, she found ways to defraud her employer at her part-time job to get extra money. Jesse was caught, fired, and about to go bankrupt. So, she went crying to her mother, who bailed her out again. Because Coretta did not see how she had contributed to the problem in the first place by being a permissive/overprotective/rescuing mother, she continued to make matters worse.

Jesse would have been empowered if her mother had allowed her to experience the consequences of her choices. (Note: We did not say that Coretta should impose consequences. Allowing teens to experience the consequences of their choices is very different from imposing consequences on them.) Allowing consequences can be done very respectfully. The most encouraging thing Coretta could have done would have been to show empathy, clearly set limits of how much she was willing to spend, and help Jesse brainstorm for ways of taking financial responsibility. Although this would not be easy for either of them, it would be empowering to both.

Permissiveness, overprotection, and rescuing may make you appear to be a saint—your teens may even love it. But these parenting styles don't help your teens learn to fly on their own. When you avoid overprotecting and rescuing, your teens may momentarily think you don't care; they may even accuse you of not loving them. But this doesn't last—they know better in the long run.

Think of some areas in which you may be overprotecting and rescuing, and thus robbing your children of the opportunity to develop self-reliance and the belief that they are capable. Choose some specific areas in which you can use kindness and firmness to stop this pattern. The firmness part simply requires that you stop being so permissive. The kindness part may require empathy and then time for training or problem solving or expressing your faith in them to handle the situations.

## VACILLATING PARENTING STYLES

Perhaps like many parents, you go back and forth from one short-term style to another. You may find yourself being too controlling and then switching to permissiveness out of guilt. As you read this book and try out the ideas, you'll find yourself decreasing the amount of time spent in short-term parenting and increasing the time spent in long-term parenting. You will understand why you do what you do. You will learn what works and what doesn't work when empowering teenagers. It helps to become aware of which of the styles is your present method of operation most of the time.

## NEGLECTFUL PARENTING/GIVING UP ON BEING A PARENT

This parenting style is like being a ghost or an absent other. Your teens hardly know you are around or may feel they need to parent you. Neglect and giving up on parenting is another form of short-term parenting. The neglectful parent invites children to learn:

1. "I'm not important and probably unlovable."
2. "My only choices are to give up or to find a way to belong somewhere else" (either in constructive or destructive ways).
3. "It's my fault my parent doesn't pay attention to me, so I have to be a certain way and improve myself so that I will be worthy of my parent's love. I have to prove I am lovable."

4. "I can't be a kid because someone in this house has to be responsible, so I guess it's me. I have to take care of my siblings and my parent(s)."

Although it can take many forms—some quite severe (for instance, substance abuse, emotional and psychological problems, workaholism, or complete indifference to a child's physical, emotional, or mental welfare)—many forms of neglect, such as aloofness, emotional unavailability, and lack of communication occur because of ignorance or misguided beliefs. Sometimes neglect is the result of despair—the belief that no matter what you do, you cannot make it work, so it's better to do nothing at all.

Example 1: One mother complained that her husband refused to parent her son and daughter from a previous marriage. He expected her to handle all discipline, but criticized her parenting methods. Although he complained vehemently about his stepchildren's behavior, he refused to deal directly with them. As a result, the children felt unloved and unimportant and lacked respect for this grown-up who had lived with them since they were preschool age. The stepfather was unable to see his behavior as neglectful: he provided for the family's economic welfare, advised the mother on raising her children, and coparented his younger biological child.

Fortunately the stepfather received some counseling. When he realized that he had been neglecting his stepchildren, he told them so, saying he'd made a mistake. He told them that he loved them and that they were important to him. He found ways to spend quality time with each of them. Instead of turning his back on what happened with these children (and later complaining to their mother), he involved himself in their lives by sharing his feelings and ideas directly with them and listening to theirs.

Giving up is another common form of neglect. Instead of controlling, parents simply try to ignore their child's behavior, hoping fervently that it will go away by itself. It usually doesn't. No matter how often teenagers say they want to be left alone, in reality they need and want some guidance. They still need a copilot. Even though they act as if they would like to throw you out of the plane, they feel abandoned if you go. What they want is a copilot who treats them with respect through kind and firm parenting.

Also, even if it seems that they don't hear a word you say, they do, although it might take days, weeks, or years for them to show you in ways that you will notice.

To many parents, having faith in their children and controlling their own behavior instead of their teen's behavior seems like doing *nothing*. Instead, it means *stopping the things that don't work*. Sometimes all a copilot can do is offer love and faith. And even though this may not achieve the desired short-term goals, the payoff in the long run is tremendous, for both parent and teen. For example, when one mother stopped being controlling or neglectful, she found that her son began to be more respectful. She learned that example really is the best teacher.

## KIND AND FIRM PARENTING

Kind and firm parenting—a long-term, encouraging parenting style—is the essence of this book. We call this *Positive Discipline parenting*. In every chapter we present skills for being a kind and firm Positive Discipline parent that go beyond the overview discussion in this chapter. The kind and firm parent invites children to learn that:

1. Freedom comes with responsibility.
2. Mutual respect is practiced here.
3. "I can learn valuable life skills, such as problem solving, communication, and respect for others."
4. Mistakes are opportunities to learn.
5. Family members have their own lives to live, and "I am part of the universe, not the center."
6. "My parents will hold me accountable through exploring the consequences of my choices in an atmosphere void of blame, shame, and pain."

Kind and firm parenting means being more interested in long-term results and goals than immediate short-term fixes. One of the first issues parents need to overcome if they want to move toward long-term parenting is an aversion to mistakes. Although it's human to make many mistakes during the growing process (and indeed we continue to make mistakes throughout life), we often equate mistakes with failure rather than with opportunities to learn (see Chapter 4). The following story provides an example of how Rhonda avoided the temptation to rescue her daughter and instead used kind and firm parenting to support her daughter in learning life skills.

Rhonda's daughter, Betsy, had set up an appointment with her teacher because she was upset about the way he had handled a situation in the classroom. Betsy asked her mother to come with her to the meeting. Because Rhonda was more concerned about the long-term goals of her daughter than about the situation at hand, she agreed, but said, "I'll be there with you for support, but I know that you will do a fine job of expressing your feelings to your teacher."

Rhonda stood next to Betsy as she stumbled all over her words, even though Betsy had had no trouble stating her opinions when the two had practiced in the car on the way to school. Rhonda then thanked the teacher for his time and later told Betsy how proud she had been when Betsy talked about her thoughts and feelings with her teacher. Rhonda didn't mention a word about Betsy's nervousness.

Rhonda's long-term goal is to help her daughter build courage. She knows that, as the years go by, Betsy will need to stand up for herself and state her opinions in situations that could be troublesome or abusive. If Betsy practices speaking for herself while her mother stands quietly by her side, the day will come when Betsy will have the confidence to take on situations by herself.

## CHANGING PARENTING STYLES CAN BE DIFFICULT

Changing your parenting style is almost the same as learning a completely new language. You live in a culture in which the language spoken is what we call "the conventional wisdom." The conventional wisdom these days is to micromanage children. Sometimes the term *helicopter parenting* is used to describe this popular micromanagement parenting style. Almost everyone around you follows the conventional wisdom—including most school discipline programs, which are based on a system of punishments and rewards. Very few people have a picture of what firm, kind, Positive Discipline parenting is like. When you practice a new way of parenting, you stick out like a sore thumb, and many people judge you and think you are "flaky." Even your teens might ask you to stop trying to help them to be responsible and just ground them like normal parents do, so they can get on with their lives and do what they want. Changing your parenting style requires three steps to overcome all this resistance.

The first step is to understand why it is a good idea. You have learned the "why" in this and previous chapters. Even with this understanding, it can be very difficult to change old patterns. It requires a paradigm shift—you really have to see yourself and your teens in a new and different light.

The second step is to learn effective parenting skills to replace the old patterns. This step is not as easy as it may sound. You may find yourself "reacting" to behavior challenges with methods that are familiar, even though they are not effective. You will need to forgive yourself, learn from your mistakes, and then choose to "act" by practicing your new skills. Because forgiving yourself (and your kids) for making mistakes is so important, you will learn more about this basic Positive Discipline principle in Chapter 4.

The third step is to acknowledge that letting go of control can be scary. This became evident to us during our parenting lectures and during counseling sessions with parents of teens. We would spend hours helping parents understand why the old methods don't work, teaching new parenting skills, and talking about how control is an illusion. Heads would be nodding in agreement, yet someone would eventually ask, "But what do I do about _____?" Inwardly, we would groan and think, *Can't they see that we've gone over at least six parenting tools that would be very effective for that situation?* Of course, we wouldn't say this out loud, but the question would always cause us to ponder, *Why don't they get it?* Obviously we can forget that change is not easy. It takes time to absorb new ideas, lots of practice, and lots of learning from mistakes. We also realized that many parents are asking the wrong questions. As long as they are asking these questions, kind and firm parenting will not work for them.

## THE WRONG (SHORT-TERM) QUESTIONS

1. How do I make my teen "mind" me?
2. How do I make my teen understand "no"?
3. How do I get my teen to listen to me?
4. How do I get my teen to cooperate and do what I say?
5. How do I "motivate" my teen (another phrase for do what I think is best)?
6. How do I make this problem go away?
7. What is the punishment/consequence for this situation?
8. What is wrong with me that I can't remember the new tools?
9. How long is this going to take?

These questions may seem perfectly legitimate to you. If so, you are still in short-term parenting mentality. You will shift to long-term parenting mentality when the following questions become your point of reference.

## THE RIGHT (LONG-TERM) QUESTIONS

1. How do I help my teen become capable?
2. How do I get into my teen's world and support his or her developmental process?
3. How do I help my teen feel belonging and significance?
4. How do I help my teen learn social and life (cooperation) skills, such as problem-solving skills and the ability to identify feelings and communicate about those feelings in words (also known as developing a feeling-words vocabulary)?

5. How do I begin to honor that my teen has different ideas about what is best for her or him?

6. How can my teen and I use this problem as an opportunity to learn from our mistakes? How can we learn to try again instead of giving up when we make mistakes?

7. How do I learn to remind myself that change takes time?

8. How do I encourage myself that taking one step at a time is enough?

9. How do I have faith in myself and my teen?

Do the "right" questions represent what you truly want? The interesting thing about these questions is that when they are answered, there will be no need for the "wrong" questions. When teens are respectfully involved in the problem-solving process, they may not "mind you" (which wouldn't really be healthy anyway), but they will be more likely to cooperate. They are likely to find inner motivation from your encouragement rather than rebelling against your control. And remember, teens are more likely to listen when they feel listened to and when you use the skills that invite listening.

Instead of struggling against problems as if they were stumbling blocks, what an empowering gift it would be for you and your teen to see them as opportunities to learn. Once you realize this, you'll save time and energy that many parents waste in trying to save their children from making mistakes.

The more uncomfortable you feel, the better you are doing. You may feel comfortable punishing, rescuing, or overprotecting because you are used to it and believe that it is right. But what are you and your teen learning from this experience? On the other hand, you will probably feel very uncomfortable saying, "No, you can't have money for skiing," or, "I'm uncomfortable about you coming home so late last night, and I want to talk with you about it." Betsy's mom had been very uncomfortable watching her daughter's struggle and had been tempted many times to jump in and rescue her daughter from an awkward situation. But she didn't jump in, because her desire to build courage in Betsy was stronger than her need to relieve Betsy's feelings at the moment.

Kind and firm parenting may feel uncomfortable to you because you may not experience the immediate results that often occur with short-term parenting. Sometimes it may feel as if you are letting your teen get away with something. When your actions relate to your long-term goals, it requires a leap of faith and a deep understanding of the long-term results to feel confident that you're doing a good job of parenting. We have worked with countless parents who have not had the chance to see the results of their efforts until a year or two down the road. Talk about faith!

## WILL CHILDREN RAISED WITH POSITIVE DISCIPLINE STILL REBEL?

Many parents have developed the mistaken belief that if they use Positive Discipline principles with their young children, their children won't make mistakes as teenagers. On the contrary, children who were raised democratically and respectfully are often more confident about risking, rebelling, and learning.

Let's assume you've been using the firm and kind model of parenting since your children were young. You've used problem-solving skills in family meetings, and your children have become very responsible and cooperative. You have a great relationship with them and are convinced they can go through adolescence smoothly. Not true. A teenager has to be a teenager.

There is no technique in the world that can tame hormones or change brain development. And when those hormones start jumping around, your children will begin their adolescent developmental tasks.

Don't panic. Your child's teen years are not the time to question everything you are learning and to wonder, "What if this Positive Discipline stuff doesn't work?" You may tell yourself that you should give more lectures on morality, spend more time setting goals for your children, and take more control so your kids won't be so inconsiderate and disrespectful now. You may wonder if you should tighten the reins before it's too late. This is not an easy time for any parent, but we can guarantee that things will not get better through tightening the reins or using punishment and control to "motivate" your teen. In fact, using these methods makes things worse.

It may help to know that children raised under the Positive Discipline model often feel freer to rebel under their parents' noses instead of going underground or waiting until they go to college. They may even use many of the messages you gave them to fuel their rebellion, such as, "But I thought you told me you wanted me to think for myself and listen to my inner voice," and, "Why are you so upset? You always taught me that mistakes are opportunities to learn. We can fix the dented fender."

## INFORM YOUR TEEN WHEN YOU CHANGE YOUR PARENTING STYLE

When you decide to use firm and kind parenting and to change your relationship with your teen, give notice. You'll be changing your role dramatically, and your teen needs to know what to expect. Giving up punishment or rescuing is a major change, so be sure to explain this to your teen. Acknowledge that you made a mistake, that punishment and rescuing doesn't work, and that you plan to change. Given that you've probably made a lot of pronouncements in the past that you didn't follow through on, your teen will most likely watch to see if you really do anything different.

Our goal is to help parents develop the courage and the skills for kind and firm parenting so that their children can develop the courage it takes to be a responsible adult. The growing process can be an enriching experience for both parents and teens.

### KIND AND FIRM PARENTING SKILLS TO REMEMBER

1. Use long-term parenting, instead of control or permissiveness, to help your teens become more responsible, self-reliant, and capable.

2. When tempted to control, ask yourself, "Will this work in the long run?" If not, use kind and firm parenting instead.

3. Although it may be more comfortable for you to micromanage your child's life, it doesn't get the job of *growing adults* done. Allow your teen to manage him- or herself.

4. When you understand why it's a good idea to change your parenting style, when you replace outdated skills with more effective ones, and when you accept that it is scary to let go of control, you are on your way to accomplishing more of what you want with your teen.

5. Help your teens balance freedom with responsibility by giving them more room to learn from their mistakes.

6. Focus on the big picture and remind yourself that parenting out of fear stunts growth. You don't have to parent perfectly.

7. Take time to cool off so you have the chance to help your children learn and grow.

### Practical Application Activity

1. Think of a recent time when you were more interested in the short-term goal of controlling your teenager (a time when you were probably acting from your reptilian brain). Describe the situation in your journal.

2. Think of how you could handle the same situation in a more rational way that would help your teen learn some skills to prepare him or her for adulthood. Write it down. This will help you be prepared for the next encounter.

3. Are there some ways in which you are being too permissive with your teen? If so, explain in your journal.

4. Think of skills to use that would start the weaning process to help your teen become self-reliant. Write them down.

5. Think of a time when you rescued your teen so that he or she would not have to experience the consequences of his or her choices. Describe it in detail.

6. What will you do the next time you are tempted to rescue your teen? How can you kindly and firmly teach your teen some important life skills?

7. Try to think of a situation in which you may be neglecting your teen out of frustration or inadequacy (or due to workaholism, substance abuse, emotional issues, or any other reason). Describe in your journal the effect this is having on your teen.

8. What are you willing to do differently to improve your relationship with your teen and with yourself? Write down specific actions you will take.

# 4

# HOW CAN MISTAKES BE WONDERFUL OPPORTUNITIES TO LEARN?

## BEING EXCITED ABOUT MISTAKES

When did mistakes get such a bad reputation? Mistakes are a natural part of growing and learning. When do we start feeling self-conscious about mistakes? When do we start hearing that mistakes mean we are inadequate, rather than finding out that mistakes are part of the learning process? Our perceptions about mistakes are shaped in a large part by the messages children receive from adults.

Sometimes negative messages about mistakes are overt: "Bad girl. You shouldn't touch the vase. You shouldn't talk in kindergarten." We are sure you can think of many other warnings about the possibility of mistakes. The truth is that she's not "bad" for touching the vase; she wouldn't be a normal toddler if she didn't want to touch it. We find it appalling that kindergarten children get "red cards" for talking in some schools. It is developmentally normal for young children to want to talk when they are excited about learning—both socially and academically.

Sometimes the messages are subtle. How much damage is done to budding self-confidence and the joy of learning when you send your children off to school or to play saying, "Be careful" or "Be good"? By saying these things, the negative connotation about mistakes is implied. Imagine the different message that would be conveyed by saying, "Enjoy your adventures today and see how much you can learn from your mistakes." This creates a climate of freedom in which to learn and grow without any loss of self-esteem from the numerous mistakes that will always be part of living.

## BEING A CHEERLEADER DURING TOUGH TIMES

Where did parents ever get the crazy idea that in order to make kids do better, they first have to make them feel worse? People cannot feel bad and learn anything positive at the same time. The best learning takes place when people feel good. If you berate your children for their mistakes, they will simply feel bad and be unable to learn from them. But if you can change your attitude and see mistakes as wonderful opportunities to learn and try again, your kids might approach things differently in the future and have more faith in themselves.

The problem about mistakes is that they happen without warning so you can't plan for them, but you can still learn from them. We suggest you start a regular ritual of having everyone at the dinner table share a mistake and what they learned from it—every day.

It will be hard to watch your children make mistakes, especially big ones, unless you have a lot of faith in your kids and yourself. Can you trust yourself to be the kind of parent who can offer support when your kid messes up instead of a load of guilt, shame, recriminations, and punishment?

It's not always easy to figure out how to maintain that, "Come on, you can do it! Hooray, that's wonderful!" attitude when your teen is making one mistake after another. You don't run to write in the baby book the first night your son or daughter comes home drunk. You don't feel encouraging when you've just spent a bundle on braces and your teen won't wear a retainer. When your teen fails a class because she spent all her time on Facebook or her Xbox instead of doing homework, you probably don't feel like calling her grandparents to brag—even though when she was little and she dropped her food off the high chair for the dog to eat, you would call them right away. Back then, instead of scolding her for age-appropriate behavior, you probably put a big piece of plastic under her chair. It doesn't seem as cute when your teen wants to spend every waking moment texting to friends, even though this is also age-appropriate behavior.

Your job at this stage of your teenager's life is to help him or her learn from mistakes with encouragement and support rather than with hand-slapping and punishment.

Teens might be willing to share some of their mistakes with you if they are certain they will not be criticized or punished. They might even avoid some mistakes if they feel safe to explore possibilities with their parents. However, most teens learn to hide their mistakes to avoid parental judgment and wrath. Or they learn to hide their behaviors that they don't think of as mistakes so they can avoid parents' lectures and control.

## CURIOSITY QUESTIONS

One of the most common mistakes parents make is that they talk, talk, talk, tell, tell, tell. When children make a mistake, most parents tell their children what happened, what caused it to happen, how they should feel about it, and what they should do about it. Then they add some kind of punishment, "to teach them a lesson." Parents would be more effective if they would stop telling and start asking.

One of my (Jane Nelsen) favorite examples of curiosity questions occurred when my youngest daughter, Mary, announced to me that she was planning to get drunk at her ninth-grade graduation party. Although I was tempted, I did not say, "Oh no you aren't! Don't you know how dangerous that is? Do you want to ruin your life? If you do, you'll be grounded for a month and you'll lose all your privileges."

Instead, I took a deep breath and said, "Tell me more about that. Why are you thinking of doing this?"

> MARY: Lots of kids are doing it, and it looks like they are having
> fun.
> ME: What do the kids say about you now because you don't
> drink?

Mary thought about that. (You know you are asking a curiosity question when kids *get* that you are truly curious and you can watch their thinking wheels turn.)

> MARY: They are always telling me they admire me and are proud
> of me.
> ME: Don't they try to pressure you to drink?
> MARY: Not really. They sometimes try to get me to drink, but
> they don't pressure me when I say no. I've just decided that I
> think I want to try it.
> ME: What do you think your friends will say about you after
> you get drunk?
> MARY: Hmmmm. They'll probably be disappointed in me.
> ME: How do you think you'll feel about yourself?

MARY [after a long, thinking pause]: I'll probably feel like a loser. [Another pause]: I guess I won't do it.

ME: Sounds like a good decision. I have faith in you to think about what you really want your life to be like instead of following the crowd. (Okay, so I did get a little lecture in there, but I don't think she heard it as a lecture.)

Curiosity questions help children *explore* the consequences of their choices instead of having consequences (punishment) *imposed* on them. Many years later, Mary told me she did try drinking a few times but didn't really like it and decided she didn't want drinking to be part of her life. Her friends told her she would get used to it, but she thought, *Why should I?*

Helping your children think for themselves is much better that inviting them to sneak and rebel. Not all children will decide to eliminate all drinking from their lives. After all, most of their parents are social drinkers (if not alcoholics). Wouldn't it be better to help teens think about

the difference between responsible and irresponsible drinking?

Curiosity questions are effective only when you are truly curious about what your children are thinking, feeling, and learning. This can be difficult when you are upset. Wait until you have calmed down before engaging in curiosity questions. It can be effective to say, "I'm too upset about this right now, but I love you and want to get together with you when I have calmed down." Sometimes it is best to put the problem on a family meeting agenda and let the whole family in on the discussion and then brainstorm for solutions.

## MODEL HOW TO LEARN FROM MISTAKES

As you grow and increase your awareness as a parent, you'll discover that many things you've done in the past were ineffective and were possibly even discouraging to your children. Your teens aren't the only ones who can learn from mistakes. You can, too. Your teens do the best they can, given their experience, knowledge, support systems, and developmental process. And so do you. One of the best ways to teach children that mistakes are wonderful opportunities to learn is to practice this principle yourself. When you make mistakes, you can feel inadequate and humiliated and think you are a failure or you can look for the opportunities to learn. The "Four R's of Recovery from Mistakes" can help you when your mistakes involve other people.

## THE FOUR R'S OF RECOVERY FROM MISTAKES

1. Recognition
2. Responsibility
3. Reconciliation
4. Resolution

**Recognition:** Recognition means awareness that you made a mistake. It is not helpful to see yourself as a failure and to wallow in blame and shame, but rather simply to realize that what you did was ineffective.

**Responsibility:** Responsibility means seeing what part you played in the mistake (maybe you invited rebellion or were discouraging in some way) and being willing to do something about it.

**Reconciliation:** Reconciliation means telling your teen that you're sorry if you treated her disrespectfully or hurt her in any way. Have you noticed how quickly kids say, "That's okay," as soon as you apologize? They are very forgiving.

**Resolution:** Resolution means working with your teen to come up with a solution that is satisfactory to both of you. Once you've recognized your mistake, taken responsibility for it, and apologized, you have usually created an atmosphere conducive to resolving the problem.

## THE FOUR R'S OF RECOVERY FROM MISTAKES IN ACTION

One day my daughter, Mary, was bugging me while I was at a salon having my hair done. She kept asking for money, wondering how much longer I was going to be, and interrupting my conversation with the beautician every five minutes.

When we finally got home, I was so angry that I called her a spoiled brat. She retorted, "Well, don't tell me later that you're sorry!" (She was familiar with the "Four R's of Recovery from Mistakes.")

I was in my primitive brain and said, "You don't have to worry, because I'm not!"

She stormed off to her room and slammed the door. I realized (recognition) that I'd made a mistake calling her a spoiled brat. (I had made many mistakes during this episode, but that was enough to start with.) I went to her room to apologize, but she wasn't ready to hear me. She was busy underlining passages in *Positive Discipline*.

She said, "You're a phony! You teach other parents to be respectful to their kids and then you call me a name."

She was right. I felt very guilty and quietly left the room. At first, I did not see my mistake as an opportunity to learn. Instead, I was thinking I should give up my career because I can't practice what I preach.

Within five minutes my daughter came to me, gave me a hug, and said, "I'm sorry."

I said, "Honey, I'm sorry, too. When I called you a spoiled brat, I was being a spoiled brat (responsibility and reconciliation). I was so angry at you for not controlling your behavior when I didn't control my own behavior."

She said, "That's okay. I really was being a spoiled brat."

"Yeah," I said, "but I can see how I provoked your behavior by not being respectful to you."

She said, "Yes, but I did interrupt you and bug you."

And that is the way it so often goes when we're willing to take responsibility for our part in creating a problem: our children learn from our example and take responsibility for their part. My daughter and I resolved the problem (resolution) by deciding that next time we would make a plan before I went into the salon. I would tell her how long I'd be, she would decide what she wanted to do during that time, and we'd meet when we were both done.

I could have wallowed in guilt about not practicing what I preached. Instead, my daughter and I both learned a valuable lesson.

## USING MISTAKES TO UNDERSTAND CONSEQUENCES AND ACCOUNTABILITY

Instead of perpetuating feelings of judgment and guilt by focusing on the mistake itself, you will teach your children infinitely more if you help them evaluate their thoughts and feelings about their decision, and what they might do differently to achieve a different result next time. You can use this same process to evaluate your own mistakes.

Becky, a parent at one of the teen workshops, asked:

> *What could I have done? I know I made a mistake. My sixteen-year-old daughter doesn't focus on her schoolwork. She said she's content to get C's, but if she doesn't raise her grades, she'll never get to go away to college, especially the college of her choice. I told her she couldn't do anything else until she does all her homework and I check it to make sure it's done and done correctly. She agreed, but when it came time to check, she explained that she had a hard time focusing and just couldn't get the work done. She could have a focus problem, but I think she says that to get me off her back.*
>
> *I told her, "Don't think you can get away with that with me, young lady. You'll sit at the table and do your work or you won't go to your friend's house." She sat at the table doodling on her paper for almost an hour and was sullen and miserable. We were all miserable. Later, she left me a note saying, "I feel no love at all for you." I know I did*

*it all wrong. I can see that I certainly didn't use kind and firm parenting by threatening her, but I don't know what else I could have done.*

The facilitator responded:

> *Remember, mistakes are wonderful opportunities to learn, so let's not think of this situation as "wrong." Instead, see it as an opportunity to discover what you really wanted to happen, what did happen, what caused it to happen, and what you could do differently next time.*

Becky and the facilitator then went through the following questions to review the situation for a better solution.

FACILITATOR: Why did you want your daughter to get better grades?

BECKY: It's important to me that she has the opportunity to go away to school, because I never did and I think I missed out. I don't want her to miss out.

FACILITATOR: Do you think she got that message, especially that you don't want her to miss out?

BECKY: Well, no.

FACILITATOR: Let's store that information for now. We'll come back to it when we get to suggestions. Why do you think she is satisfied with C's if she could do better?

BECKY: I think she is sure that the college she wants to attend counts more on service to the community than grades, and she's involved in tons of service projects.

FACILITATOR: Have you ever felt that way, wanting to put your focus where you thought it was most important?

BECKY: Yes. I can understand that.

FACILITATOR: Can you see how you skipped the issues that were important to you and your daughter and got into a power struggle that escalated into a revenge cycle?

BECKY: Yes. I felt bad after threatening to make her miss going to her friends, especially because I know the girls were going to work on making a list of places they could collect donations for the school fund-raiser, but I couldn't let her get away with talking to me like that. So I won the round, but she sure got back at me. I was very hurt and frustrated when I got her note.

FACILITATOR: Based on the issues we've brought to the surface, can you think of any principles and strategies we've discussed in the workshop that might apply to this situation?

BECKY: No. I feel really stuck. I can't imagine what logical consequence I could have used.

FACILITATOR: Great! If you can't think of one, it probably means a logical consequence is not appropriate in this case. As I've mentioned before, most of us are so enamored with the idea of consequences that we often try to apply them when they aren't appropriate, or we try to disguise a punishment by calling it a logical consequence. How about making sure the message of love gets through, sharing what you want, getting into her world to find out what she wants, and then working out a plan where you both win? Would you like to role-play all that to see what it feels like?

BECKY: Sure.

FACILITATOR: Okay. Would you like to play your daughter and I'll play the mom?

BECKY: Yes. That feels easier to me right now.

FACILITATOR: Start with what your daughter said in the beginning.

BECKY/DAUGHTER: Mom, it's not important to me to get better than C's in those classes.

FACILITATOR/MOM: It's really important to me that your grades are good enough for you to get into the college you want.

BECKY/DAUGHTER: Me, too, but I googled the college entrance requirements and service counts for more than grades, and I have a ton of service projects on my admission form.

FACILITATOR/MOM: Well, I'm happy to hear that you've been studying the admission requirements. It helps me to know that getting into that college is important to you. I would hate for you to miss out because of some C's that you could have turned into B's or A's. Would it be okay with you if I set up an appointment with our college coach to run this by her and see if she agrees with your research? She's helped a lot of kids get into colleges, and I'm sure she's dealt with your college of choice in the past and would know firsthand if what they say is what they really do. Then we could discuss this at our next family meeting so we can work out a plan to accomplish both our goals?

BECKY/DAUGHTER: Sure. Thanks, Mom.

FACILITATOR: How are you feeling now as the daughter?

BECKY: I feel loved and respected and willing to work on a plan with you at the family meeting.

FACILITATOR: It sounds to me like you're now on a track that sidesteps the power struggles and revenge cycles. This track is more likely to get everyone what he or she wants while teaching perceptions and skills that will be useful to your daughter.

The following is a list of the perceptions and skills that help parents to improve understanding and communication after making the kinds of mistakes that lead to power struggles, rebellion, and revenge:

## SIX STEPS FOR CORRECTING MISTAKES

1. Get back to the spirit of the rule rather than the letter of the rule. (The spirit was helping her get into the college of her choice. The letter of the rule was do your homework or be punished.)
2. Treat children the way you would like to be treated—with understanding, dignity, and respect. (How would you like it if

someone threatened to punish you simply because you wanted to do what you thought was best?)

3. Share what is important to you and why. (Make sure the message of love and respect comes through.)
4. Find out what is important to your child and why.
5. Be willing to make exceptions to rules. (This is not the same as being permissive.)
6. Make an appointment (family meeting or some other time) to work on a plan to meet the needs and desires of all involved, without forming a pattern of exceptions.

When you find yourself involved in a conflict that creates distance between you and your teenager, ask yourself, "Am I acting from my fear and anger or from my love and faith?" Then use these six steps to correct your mistakes and help you remember the kind and firm parenting skills that will be encouraging to both of you.

## KIND AND FIRM PARENTING SKILLS TO REMEMBER

1. Tell your teen often that mistakes are wonderful opportunities to learn.
2. Have faith in your teenager to make decisions and to learn from mistakes.
3. Help your teenagers explore the consequences of their choices through friendly *what* and *how* questions.
4. Teens are young people with feelings and should be treated with understanding, dignity, and respect.
5. Share what is important to you and why. (Make sure the message of love and respect comes through.)
6. Find out what is important to your child and why.
7. Be willing to make exceptions to rules. (This is not the same as being permissive.)
8. Instead of trying to parent on the fly, make a date or wait for the family meeting to work out a plan that all can live with.

*Practical Application Activity*

Take a deep breath. Ask your teen for his or her help. Put on your curiosity hat and good listening ears. Now ask your teen to give you an example of a mistake they think you've made as a parent. Use the "Four R's of Recovery from Mistakes" and either write down your answers to each of the R's or discuss your answers with your teen. The four R's are Recognition, Responsibility, Reconciliation, and Resolution.

# 5

# HOW DO YOU
# MOTIVATE TEENS?

## YES, IT IS POSSIBLE!

**W**hen parents ask, "How do I motivate my teen?," they usually mean, "How do I get my teens to do what I want? How do I get her to have some balance in her life? How do I get him off the computer, to get outside, or to do just about anything except sitting around doing nothing?"

Encouragement is the key to motivation. Every parenting tool we are sharing in this book is designed to encourage and motivate teens. In this chapter, we'll cover six surefire teen motivators: compliments, humor, let's make a deal/collateral, motivation through involvement, joint problem solving, and follow-through.

## COMPLIMENTS

People do better when they feel better. There's nothing like getting a compliment for something you feel good about or being affirmed for who you are to improve motivation. This is true for everyone, but especially for teens, who often hear endless criticism, nagging, and complaining about their poor performance. If you're used to using praise as a motivator, you may have a tough time finding something praiseworthy with your teen. That's why we suggest encouragement, because it works even when your kids are in the dumps and making mistakes.

One place to make sure everyone gets a compliment or appreciation is the family meeting (discussed in detail in Chapter 7). If you have weekly meetings and start each meeting with something positive, your teens might want to be at the meeting for that alone. A fifteen-year-old boy said his favorite time of the week was at the family meeting when he got appreciation/compliments.

During the week, look for ways to let your kids know how unique they are, what you appreciate about them, how adorable they were as little kids. Tell them stories about what they used to do when they were younger. Ask them if there's something they wish people would say about them or like about them or notice about them, and then make sure you tell them exactly what they want to hear. They will like hearing it, even if they told you what they wanted.

## HUMOR

Teenagers enjoy a sense of humor and respond to it much better than to lectures and nagging. The following situations illustrate how parents use humor to invite cooperation and to lighten things up.

When a teenage girl forgot to set the table, her mother served the dinner directly onto the table. Everyone laughed at the absurdity of the situation. The table was set on time from then on.

Peter was a father of three teens who used betting and guessing games to motivate the children and add humor to a situation. When Peter noticed the chores weren't getting done as agreed, he'd say, "Someone forgot to do something they agreed to. I'll give a dollar to the first person who guesses what it is." The teens ran around the house trying to find out who the culprit was so they could win a dollar.

Another time Peter said, "I'll bet two dollars you can't finish your yard work before the football game starts." He was effective using bets and games because they were infrequent and unexpected. Had Peter tried using bets as rewards and bribes, his children would have felt less respected because he would have implied that the only reason his teens helped the family was for the money.

One day at the grocery store, in the same spirit of fun, Peter tore the shopping list in half and gave one part to his son and the other to his friend. Peter said, "I'll take you two for pizza if you can find everything on your half of the list in fifteen minutes. Go!" Shoppers watched in surprise as the two teens ran through the store throwing items into their carts.

Sometimes a sense of humor is the only way to get things done. When Sharon's fifteen-year-old stepson, Cole, moved in with the family, it wasn't long before his presence became known in the household. First, Sharon's hairbrush disappeared, then half the kitchen towels, and finally, several blankets. He paced, twisted, twirled, and danced as he talked on the phone until the cord was a tangle of knots. Cole left his dirty dishes, magazines, and soda cans in Sharon's bedroom, where he lay on her bed each day after school to watch Sharon's TV because his room was too messy. The final straw came one day when Sharon started to set the table and couldn't find any silverware in the drawer or her kitchen scissors to cut up some herbs.

"Cole Peter Anderson," Sharon yelled, "come here this minute!" Cole sauntered in and asked, "What are you so uptight about? Did you have a bad day at work?" Sharon clenched her fists and was ready to read Cole the riot act, when she decided to try another approach. She knew Cole was very defiant and masterful at defeating adults who told him what to do or got angry when he didn't do what they wanted.

Sharon paused for a moment and then asked, "Cole, have you read your horoscope today?"

"Sharon, what are you talking about? I don't read the horoscopes. You know that."

"Well, listen to this," said Sharon, as she opened the morning paper and began reading with a serious face. "This is what it says for Aires. Today is the day you will feel an irresistible urge to return Sharon's scissors to the kitchen, bring all the dirty dishes and silverware back to be washed, untangle the phone cord so it reaches to the table, and put Sharon's hairbrush back in her bathroom."

"Let me see that. I think you're kidding me, Sharon," said Cole, as he grabbed for the paper.

"You run and take care of those things and I'll cut it out for you to read later," Sharon teased. Cole grinned from ear to ear and said, "Sharon, you're weird." A few minutes later he brought a laundry basket filled with dirty dishes into the kitchen, replaced the scissors, and started working on the phone cord. Sharon walked over and gave Cole a big hug and said, "Thanks, guy!"

On another occasion Sharon asked Cole if he would like help with his procrastination. "Sharon, it's a family trait. All the guys in our family do it. It's in our blood."

"Well, I have an idea about how you could change it if you want to, but I'm not going to tell you unless you beg me."

"OK, Sharon, I'm begging. Please, please, please, what's your idea?" Cole joked.

"Do you know that most actions have a beginning, middle, and an end? I notice that you are good at beginnings, fair with middles, and lousy with ends. Either you could get a business card that says 'Cole Anderson, Procrastinator, No Job Too Small to Put Off,' or you could try my ABC Happiness Plan."

Cole asked, "What's an ABC Happiness Plan?"

"I can't tell you, but I can show you. Are you ready?" asked Sharon. Cole knew he was being tricked once again, but Sharon had a way of helping him save face and make things fun, so he decided to go along with her. "OK, Sharon, I'm ready."

"We'll start with 'A.' Go to your car and bring in all the towels and blankets that belong in the house." Cole ran out the door to his car and returned with his arms loaded. "What next, Sharon?"

"Here comes 'B.' Take all the towels and blankets in your arms and put them in the washer, add soap, and start the machine. Then stand in front of the machine and see if you can guess what 'C' will be."

"I suppose 'C' is that I'm supposed to fold the stuff and put it away," mused Cole.

"Clever boy. I knew you'd catch on to the ABC Happiness Plan. Aren't you feeling happy? I know that I am," Sharon said, laughing. Cole just shook his head and gave Sharon that special look that said adults can be pretty strange.

Sharon could have turned any of these situations into a confrontation, insisting Cole was being lazy and defiant. She made a decision about whether she wanted to live in harmony or in a war zone. The more she relied on her humor, the more Cole pitched in without a battle.

## LET'S MAKE A DEAL AND USING COLLATERAL

Like humor, teens relate to making a deal. It's another version of give-and-take, a concept that appeals to a teen's sense of fairness and logic. Since teens can be so self-centered and expect the world to revolve around them, making deals can motivate teens when all else fails.

There are good deals and bad deals. Bad deals are those that you can't follow through on or that are unrealistic or age/skill/life experience inappropriate. The age-old deal "We'll get a dog if you promise to take care of it" is an example of a bad deal. Most kids get tired of taking care of a pet within weeks of getting one, and by then you are too bonded to take the dog to a shelter.

A good deal would be, "If you walk the dog for me on weekdays, I'll do a special favor for you on weekends." That deal could be a bad deal if you aren't around to see that the dog is getting walked. Here's another example of bad deal/good deal. "You can take the car tonight if you promise to fill it with gas." That's a bad deal because your teen has already gotten the car so there's no leverage. A good deal would be, "If you wash the car before you leave, you can use it tonight."

Here are some other good deals. "I won't bug you during the week about getting chores done as long as you finish all of them by Wednesday dinner. If they aren't done by dinnertime, I'll hold dinner till you get them done." That deal can work if you can live with that type of deadline and if you are home for Wednesday dinner to follow through. Another good deal is, "I'll make you a deal. I'll pick you and your friends up from the movie if you can find another parent to take you there." How about, "I'll make you a deal. I'll match whatever you save for that new sweater (guitar, game, etc.)"?

Collateral works really well with teens. If they want to borrow something of yours, they need to give you collateral that you will return when they return the item. Good collateral might be a favorite piece of clothing, an iPod, an iPad, a cell phone, and so on. It needs to be an item that has value to your teen.

## MOTIVATION THROUGH INVOLVEMENT

Dana shared the following at a parenting class: "My daughter, Sage, is doing exceptionally well in school. She is getting the highest score on most tests, and she is not feeling challenged. At the last parent-teacher conference she asked for more challenging work from her teacher." Other members of the group wanted to know what Dana did to motivate Sage to do so well.

Dana then shared the following: "I have learned that what works well with Sage is explaining to her the benefit of doing well. I use every opportunity I can to point that out to her. When she learns something new, I take it to the next level with more information and then point out to her that is what is so cool about learning, that you learn one new thing and it opens up a whole new world.

"For example, when she learned about the planets, I said, 'Some people believe there are more planets that we don't even know about yet.' That prompted more questions from her, and soon we were searching for answers online because I didn't know the answers.

"And as the saying goes, 'Our children learn more from our actions than our words,' so I have tried to show her my love of learning by reading, by taking classes on something I want to learn about, and by making her homework a priority.

"We have a motto, 'work before play,' and we have had to work on that. She has learned that it is better to get the work done first so she doesn't have to stress at the last minute. With her book reports, for example, we get the book at the first of the month, count the number of pages in the book, and determine how many she needs to read a night so she has the weekend before the report is due to get it done. My goal is showing her it's really not hard if you do a little here and there. I think we all get discouraged when we are doing it last minute and we are stressed; it takes the fun out of it. Showing her it's really not that hard has helped her love it!

"Maybe most important is that I have found that I need to be engaged with her while she does her homework because she gets very sidetracked. If I walk away, I find her playing with her eraser, or checking herself out in the mirror—things like that! So I sit beside her at the table or I cook while she is at the kitchen island, then I help her stay focused and I can help answer questions. It takes a lot of work, but it is rewarding for me so I enjoy being able to be this strong influence in her life to help her get off to a good start.

"Now she doesn't need my oversight as much. For example, a couple of weeks ago she was at a Halloween party until 10:00 p.m. and was trying to get Super Reader at school (where you read every day for a month). So she came home late and read so she didn't miss that day (without me saying anything and with me exhausted falling asleep beside her). Another day, she stayed up late to get all her assignments done because now it's important to her to do well. She owned it, not me!

"To sum it all up, I think it takes teaching them to love to learn and dedication/involvement on a parent's part. I am a firm believer in the theory that parent involvement is the key to a child's success!"

Dana shared the kind of motivation that is very supportive without nagging, bribing, demanding, or punishing. Dana's involvement included working *with* Sage, not *to* or *at* Sage. The proof of her success is that by spending quality time and follow-through in the beginning, Sage has adopted the habits and can now do them on her own.

## JOINT PROBLEM SOLVING WORKS WITH TEENS

Willie saved all his birthday and Christmas money from the time he was five, telling everyone that one day he would buy himself a really cool car. When Willie got his license, he told his folks he was going car shopping. His parents stopped in their tracks and said, "No way. You just got your license, and you're not ready to have a car of your own." "But I've been saving my whole life, and you never told me that before," Willie complained. "That's not fair, and you can't stop me. It's my money."

What a perfect opportunity for Willie and his folks to sit down and use the "Four Steps for Joint Problem Solving."

### FOUR STEPS FOR JOINT PROBLEM SOLVING

1. Teen shares his or her issues and goals.
2. Parent shares his or her issues and goals.
3. If goals of teen and parent are far apart, they brainstorm to find options.
4. Teen and parent pick an option they can both live with and try it out for a short time.

When Willie and his folks followed the process, Willie's issues were that he had waited forever and wanted his own car so he could experience the results of his years of effort. He wanted it to look a certain way, drive a certain way, and he planned to keep it perfect. He didn't want to share. His folks were worried that if he had his own car, he would think it was okay to go anywhere he wanted without checking in with them. They were also concerned that he'd let his schoolwork slip because he was spending too much time in his car, on his car, and working to afford having a car. After much brainstorming, they decided that it was fine for Willie to buy the car as long as he agreed to continue to check in with them about where he was going and how often he'd be using the car. If his homework slipped, he agreed to give his folks the car keys until he caught up.

It is likely that Willie would give up the keys without too much fuss because of his agreement. However, even though Willie was respectfully involved in joint problem solving, it is not likely that he would be the first to suggest that he should relinquish his keys. It would most likely require follow-through.

## FOLLOW-THROUGH

The teen motivators we have discussed so far are fairly quick and easy. Follow-through is more complicated and requires more guidance on the part of parents, but it is worth the effort because it is a surefire method that really helps teens keep their agreements. Follow-through is an excellent alternative to authoritarian methods or permissiveness. With follow-through, you can meet the needs of the situation while maintaining dignity and respect for all concerned. Follow-through is also a way to help teens learn the life skills they need in order to feel good about themselves while learning to be contributing members of society.

Before showing you how to follow through, however, we will try to convince you to stop using what doesn't work—logical consequences.

Too many parents think that teens should experience a logical consequence when they don't keep their agreements. Not so. Most logical consequences are poorly disguised punishments that do not fool teens. If it looks like a punishment, sounds like a punishment, and feels like a punishment, it is a punishment even if it is called a "logical consequence." We say "most" logical consequences are poorly disguised punishments because logical consequences can be truly logical and helpful.

Because the use of logical consequences has become one of the more popular parenting methods today, it may be difficult to accept what we have to say about using them with teenagers. You probably won't like hearing that most logical consequences are usually ineffective with teenagers. Because the main life tasks for teens involve testing their power, they see the use of logical consequences as a method to control them. Once you realize how teens view logical consequences, you will see that the concept of follow-through is more motivating.

### What Is Follow-Through?

Follow-through is a respectful, four-step approach to parenting teens that teaches cooperation, life skills, and responsibility in spite of resistance. It works whether you are trying to move your teen away from the computer, to join the family, or to keep up responsibilities to themselves and the family. The key is that follow-through involves you, because you are the only one who does the follow-through. The result is that your teen also follows through, but rarely without your participation. Think of this as one of your main copilot duties.

### THE FOUR STEPS FOR EFFECTIVE FOLLOW-THROUGH

1. Have a friendly discussion with your teen to gather information about what is happening regarding the problem. (Listen first and then share your thoughts.)

2. Brainstorm solutions with your teen. (Use your humor and throw in some exaggerations.) Choose a solution that both you and your teen can agree to. Finding one you both like may take some negotiating, because your favorite solution may be different from your teen's favorite.

3. Agree on a date and time deadline. (You will find out later why this is imperative.)

4. Understand teens well enough to know that the deadline probably won't be met and simply follow through on the agreement by kindly and firmly holding your teen accountable (example on page 77, "Follow-Through in Real Life").

Before we provide examples of effective follow-through, it is important to understand the traps that defeat follow-through.

## FOUR TRAPS THAT DEFEAT FOLLOW-THROUGH

1. Believing that teens think the way you think and have the same priorities you have.

2. Getting into judgments and criticism instead of sticking to the issue.

3. Not getting agreements in advance that include a specific time deadline.

4. Not maintaining dignity and respect for yourself and your teen.

In our workshops, to help parents learn the art of follow-through and to show them that it really does work, we often ask for a volunteer to role-play a teen who has not kept an agreement to do a task, such as mowing the lawn. We then point to the "Four Steps for Effective Follow-Through" and ask the volunteer to pretend we have already gone through them as a parent and a teen. To set up the role-play, we ask the teen to sit in a chair and pretend he or she is playing a video game. The deadline has arrived, but the task is not done. We then role-play the adult who follows through by using the following "Four Hints for Effective Follow-Through."

## FOUR HINTS FOR EFFECTIVE FOLLOW-THROUGH

1. Keep comments simple, concise, and friendly. ("I notice you didn't do your task. Would you please do that now?")
2. In response to objections, ask, "What was our agreement?"
3. In response to further objections, shut your mouth and use nonverbal communication. (Point to your watch after every argument. Smile knowingly. Give a hug and point to your watch again.) It helps to understand the concept of "less is more." The less you say, the more effective you will be. The more you say, the more ammunition you give your kids for an argument—which they will win every time.
4. When your teen concedes (sometimes with great annoyance), say, "Thank you for keeping our agreement."

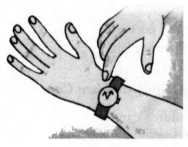

One thing we ask of the volunteer role-playing the teen is to be in the present moment. By this we mean the volunteer should respond to what is being done now rather than responding in ways that a teen would react to disrespectful methods. When the volunteer does this, it is amazing how quickly the "teen" comes to agreement (after a little resistance).

Many parents object and say, "My teen would not give in that quickly." We disagree and show them why by referring to the "Four Traps That Defeat Follow-Through" and asking the volunteer teen the following questions:

1. At any time, did you feel criticized or judged?
2. At any time, did you feel I did not maintain dignity and respect—for you and for ourselves?
3. Did I stick to the issue?
4. How much difference did it make knowing that you had agreed to a specific deadline?

The volunteer always says no to the first two questions, yes to the third question, and responds that the specific deadline made it difficult to argue for delays. The volunteer also shares that it is very effective when we stop talking and give the "look" (Hint 3 for Effective Follow-Through) with a smile that says, "Nice try, but you and I both know better."

Other parents object to follow-through because they don't think they should have to remind kids to keep their agreements. They want their kids to be "responsible" without reminders. We have five questions for these parents:

1. When you don't take time to remind them with dignity and respect, do you spend time scolding, lecturing, and punishing or doing the job for them?
2. Does this change their behavior?
3. Have you noticed how responsible your kids are about keeping agreements that are important to them?
4. Do you really think mowing the lawn and other chores are important to your kids?
5. Do you remember, without reminders, to complete everything that you have promised to do—especially when it is something you don't want to do?

Although follow-through takes time and energy, it is much more fun and productive than scolding, lecturing, and punishing. Even though chores aren't a high priority for teens, it is important that they do them. Follow-through accomplishes this goal.

### Follow-Through in Real Life
When you change your behavior, your teens will change theirs. When kids have made an agreement that includes a deadline (to the minute), they

are left with a feeling of fairness and responsibility when they are held accountable.

Thirteen-year-old Cory was not washing his clothes or changing the sheets on his bed as he'd agreed to do. Cory's mom, Jamie, said, "I'd like to talk with you about your laundry. Let's meet after dinner." When they sat down, Jamie asked Cory what his issues were about doing his laundry. She found out that he wasn't really sure how to run the machine and was afraid he would break it. Jamie shared her issues, which were that she didn't like to see him wearing dirty clothes to school and sleeping on dirty sheets.

Cory said he was willing to do his laundry but he needed help with the machine. Jamie agreed: "I'd like you to choose a day this week to meet me in the laundry room at six p.m. for a lesson. I'd also like you to choose which day of the week you'll set aside for doing your laundry and changing your sheets. With a family as large as ours, it would be best if we each have our own laundry day. I'll check back with you in an hour to see which day you've chosen."

An hour later, Cory said he guessed that Tuesday would be all right for the laundry lesson and would also be okay for his laundry day. Jamie said, "Fine. I'll see you at six on Tuesday in the laundry room."

But on Tuesday, when Jamie went to the laundry room at the agreed-upon time, Cory wasn't there. Jamie found Cory parked in front of the TV and said, "Do you remember your decision about the best time for a laundry lesson?"

Cory said, "Aw, Mom, I don't want to do it now; I'm watching this."

Jamie was very friendly but very persistent. "What was our agreement?"

Cory responded, "We agreed to six, but I'll do it later, Mom."

Jamie simply stood in front of him with a friendly but expectant look in her eye. Cory finally said, "Oh, all right! This is so stupid!"

Instead of responding to the dig, Jamie simply said, "Thank you for keeping your agreement."

Every Tuesday, Cory and his mother went through a similar routine. Jamie would say, "Remember the day you chose to do your laundry and change your sheets?" No matter what kind of arguments or put-downs Cory came up with, Jamie would simply follow through in a friendly manner while avoiding lectures and insults. She knew it would be absolutely abnormal for Cory to be excited about washing his clothes and changing his sheets. But it was important to her that he help around the house and also that he be equipped with the skills of keeping commitments. She saved them both a lot of hassles by simply getting an agreement and then following through.

Jamie gave up the notion that Cory would remember to do this job without being reminded. At thirteen, she realized Cory was thinking more about how to buy a new skateboard or how to tell his dad that he got a poor grade on his report card than about doing his laundry. She decided that follow-through once a week, as long as it didn't turn into a power struggle, was worth it. She was pleasantly surprised when Cory eventually started remembering to take care of his laundry without being reminded.

## LESSONS TEENS LEARN WHEN YOU DON'T FOLLOW THROUGH

1. They don't have to keep agreements. If you don't, why should they?
2. Your word doesn't mean anything. You're just blowing smoke. They may follow your example.
3. Manipulation works to avoid responsibility.
4. They can get away with all kinds of behavior because you don't allow them to be accountable by following through.
5. Love means getting people to "give in."

The methods we've presented in this chapter have much more chance of success than using written contracts with your teens. Most parents who use contracts find that they are rarely followed and usually too complicated for simple follow-through. Teens are willing to sign anything to get their parents off their backs. If an agreement is put in writing, it should be done in the form of a record, not a contract. A contract usually includes some kind of penalty (or punishment) if not kept. An agreement does not include penalties or punishment—just follow-through.

Even adults forget the details of agreements. When it is written down, you can always check, "Exactly what was our agreement?" Then follow-through does not become arbitrary.

Some families make decisions at family meetings and record their agreements in a notebook. Others put a note on a calendar or on the refrigerator, until the new arrangement becomes part of the normal schedule. Some written agreements take the form of a job chart. Follow-through is the most effective way to help kids and adults keep their commitments.

### Some Final Follow-Through Tips

It's easier to follow through if you train yourself and your teens in advance. By spending time working with your teens on the necessary steps to achieve the agreed-upon goals, you can make follow-through much smoother. Don't negotiate a new agreement instead of following through on the original one. You need to start and finish with the same plan. (It is okay to negotiate a different agreement during a family meeting or scheduled problem-solving session, but it is important to follow through until the agreement can be changed formally.)

Follow-through never involves threats. It allows you to keep your own power while letting your teens keep theirs. It feels good for everyone. Once you get in the habit of using follow-through, you can maintain a sense of humor when things don't go according to plan. Follow-through can be a wonderful way to enrich your relationship with your teens.

Follow-through helps parents to be proactive and thoughtful instead of reactive and inconsiderate. Once you understand that teens have their own priorities, even though they need to follow some of yours, you can see their resistance as cute, adorable, and normal instead of lazy, inconsiderate, and irresponsible. Follow-through can make parenting pleasurable, magical, and fun.

## KIND AND FIRM PARENTING SKILLS TO REMEMBER

1. You can motivate your teens with encouragement, which is very different from trying to get your teens to do what you want.

2. Humor, collateral, let's make a deal, and involvement are positive motivation tools.

3. There is one surefire way to get your kids to keep their agreements—follow-through. It may be a lot of work for you in the beginning, but it will be worth every minute of the time you spend to train both you and your teen to use better habits.

4. Read the four steps, the four traps, and the four hints for successful follow-through again and again, because they are very different from how you would normally respond as a parent—and as a human.

5. You must be there at the first deadline to set up the follow-through. It won't work in the long run without you there in the beginning.

6. If you whine or complain that using follow-through is too much work, track how much time you spend reminding and nagging your teen instead. Notice the effect that nagging has on you and on your teen. Keep a checklist of how often the task you are nagging about actually gets done. We call this a reality check.

7. Follow-through will help you use fewer words, and your kids will hear you better.

8. Don't hesitate to prepare in advance and maybe even practice with a friend. You can always listen to the "Empowering Teenagers and Yourself in the Process" mp3 for a live demonstration. It helps! (They can be found on our website at www.positivediscipline.com.)

9. We do not recommend making contracts with your teens. If you need to write down information as a reminder for both of you,

that is respectful and effective. Setting up a contract means you are treating your teenager like a client or an adversary. If you do sign a contract, don't be surprised by your teen's attitudes.

### Practical Application Activity

1. Think of a situation in which you nagged your teen (dirty dishes in the bedrooms; leaving clothes, shoes, books all over the house; smelly animal cages, etc.).
2. Refer to the four steps, the four traps, and the four hints for effective follow-through and work with your teen to set up a situation to practice for a week.

Reread this chapter every time you feel the urge to nag. (The book will probably end up well worn.)

# 6

# DOES YOUR TEENAGER HEAR ANYTHING YOU SAY?

## COMMUNICATION SKILLS

Do you and your teenager really listen to each other? What happens to all those words you use? Why won't your teen use more words and talk to you? Would your teen talk to you more if he or she felt listened to, understood, and taken seriously? In this chapter, we show you how to communicate in a way that both you and your teen feel listened to and understood. In Chapter 11, we'll focus on a different kind of teenage communication—the Internet, texting, social networking, and cell phones.

When you read the word "communication," be honest. What's the first thing you think of? We'll bet it's talking. If you're like most parents of teens, you probably do too much of that. Here's a test. The next time you start "talking" (lecturing, reminding, nagging, coaxing, etc.), look at your kids and see if they are rolling their eyes, texting a friend, or watching TV. They might be looking right at you, but you are so busy talking  that you don't notice they are "gone." If you are feeling ignored, chances are your kids *are* ignoring you. They might even be parent deaf by this time in their lives. Do you find yourself saying, "How many times do I have to tell you? Do you hear anything I have to say? This is the hundredth time I've told you." This is a huge clue that what you are doing isn't working.

Also consider what you really mean. Many parents who are complaining that their teens don't listen really mean that their teens don't obey. You're in good company, as most parents of teens do a lot of talking, and most teens do a lot of tuning out.

Newsflash: listening is the primary ingredient of communication, not talking, and it is the least developed parenting skill. When parents ask, "Why won't my child listen to me?" we ask, "Do you model for your child what listening is all about? In other words, do you listen first?"

So much has been written and said about listening that you would think most people would know how to do it, but they don't. Simply put, listening is difficult because issues keep getting in the way. People usually take everything they hear personally; they want to defend their positions, explain, correct, retaliate, or tell a better story. Parents especially get extremely "ego involved" with their kids—that is, they take things very personally. Or they keep thinking that talking is the best way to teach—even when their personal evidence shows them it doesn't work. You might want to tape a copy of the following list of barriers to listening on your bathroom mirror and read it every day until you overcome the ways you interrupt the listening process.

### BARRIERS TO LISTENING

1. Stepping in to fix or rescue so you can be a "good" parent, rather than listening as your teens try to figure things out for themselves.

2. Trying to talk teens out of their feelings or perceptions so they'll have the "right" perceptions and feelings.

3. Giving defensive explanations about your point of view.

4. Interrupting to teach lessons on morality or values.

5. Taking what teens say personally, and letting your own unresolved issues get in the way.

6. Using what your teens say against them to punish, criticize, call names, and lecture.

By rearranging the letters in the word *listen*, you can find a primary key to good listening: *silent*. Be silent when listening, because you can't talk and listen at the same time.

A group of teens were invited to create a list of the top ten tips to help parents communicate better. They came up with more than ten. Here are some of our favorites. (As you read the list, you might notice that most of these would also be good tips for your teens to improve their listening skills, but parents being the adults in the family need to change first.)

## TEENS' ADVICE TO PARENTS ON HOW TO IMPROVE COMMUNICATION

1. No lectures.
2. Make it short and sweet.
3. Don't talk down to us.
4. Listen to us—don't talk over us.
5. Don't repeat yourself.
6. If we have the guts to tell you what we did wrong, don't be mad and don't overreact.
7. Don't pry or give us the third degree.
8. Don't yell from a different room and expect us to come running.
9. Don't try to make us feel guilty by saying things like, "I did it because you couldn't find the time."

10. Don't make promises you can't keep.
11. Don't compare us with siblings or friends.
12. Don't talk to our friends about us.

The following skills are effective only when parents are sincerely interested in understanding the world of their teenagers and are willing to respect their reality.

## SKILLS TO HELP YOU LISTEN

1. Realize that the feeling behind what you do is more important than what you actually do. Being silent while you are reading the paper or thinking about something else doesn't count. Effective listening requires wide open body language to indicate your interest.
2. Have respect for separate realities. Be open to the fact that there is more than one way of seeing things. (Don't you love it when someone is that interested in you? Well, your teens like it, too.)
3. Show empathy. Say "I can understand why you might feel that way or see it that way." This doesn't mean that you see things the same way, just that you understand how your teen could come to his or her conclusions.
4. Be curious. Ask questions that will invite more information from your teen. For example, "How did that make you feel? What about that was important to you? Could you give me an example of when I made you so angry? How often do I do that? Is there anything else that is bothering you?"

The last question ("Is there anything else?") is one that deserves more exploration. Many parents have shared with us that remembering to ask that particular question again and again has done more to help them get into their teen's world and understand core issues than anything else they have done.

## "ANYTHING ELSE?" WORKING ON YOUR ATTITUDE OF CURIOSITY

Too often, parents react to the first bit of information they get, although it usually isn't even close to the key issue. Avoid the temptation to respond to the surface information and instead keep asking this question, "Is there anything else about that that bothered you? Is there anything else you want to say about that?" Keep being curious enough to elicit more and more information. It may seem awkward and phony at first, but keep practicing. Once you get over feeling clumsy, it will become more spontaneous. You'll find yourself being truly curious and interested.

Adele shared the following story about her thirteen-year-old. While she and her daughter were visiting a friend, Adele volunteered her daughter to help the friend with some babysitting. However, she neglected to check with her daughter first, a point her daughter had raised on numerous occasions. Adele meant to be more sensitive to her daughter's needs, but sometimes she forgot. On the way home, she noticed that her daughter was sullen and moody, so she asked, "What's wrong?" Her daughter said angrily, "Nothing. You're just being your usual self. You volunteered me to babysit without asking me."

Although Adele realized she had made a mistake, she could tell that her daughter needed some space before hearing any apologies. Therefore, Adele decided to wait and continue the conversation later. That evening she asked her daughter if she could sit on her bed for a while. She said, "I don't care," so Adele sat down and began stroking her daughter's hair. Tears ran down her daughter's cheek as Adele said, "Sometimes life can be so difficult, especially when we don't feel understood." After a few minutes she added, "I'm sorry that I was disrespectful of you by volunteering you for a job without asking you first. I made a mistake."

"It's not just that, Mom," she said.

"What then?" Adele asked.

"I felt too embarrassed to say no."

"Anything else?"

"I don't know how I can get my schoolwork done if I babysit after school."

"Anything else?"

"I don't like to babysit her kids because they are so difficult and never listen."

Adele nodded and said, "Thanks for letting me know your feelings. I'm willing to call and say I made a mistake if you like. Want to sleep on it?"

Her daughter said, "Okay, but maybe it will be all right. I'll let you know in the morning. Love you, Mom."

Adele demonstrated many important ideas about communication. Instead of making her daughter's moodiness a big issue by saying, "We need to talk about what happened," she waited until the situation had cooled down. Then she "hung out" by sitting on her daughter's bed. If Adele had demanded that they talk, her daughter would have taken this as a signal that a lecture or a punishment was on the way.

Adele realized how much more effective it is to live what she believed than to preach what she believed. She wanted good communication with her daughter, so she had to work at becoming a better communicator first. In the long run, using this approach will mean that teens will be much more likely to "hear" their parents' actions than they are to "hear" the lectures. Although they may seem to rebel against your example for a short time, when you quietly and respectfully live what you believe, you'll be pleased at how many of your values your children will adopt when they grow up. Adele modeled waiting for the right time to talk, apologizing for her mistake, and listening to her daughter's feelings without judgments or trying to fix or change her daughter.

## DEVELOP A FEELING-WORDS VOCABULARY

Learn to communicate from your heart and your gut using a feeling-words vocabulary. Instead of hiding feelings, help your children identify and share their feelings. You may be like many adults who don't know what feelings are and can't help their teens, who are a bundle of feelings waiting to be spoken. Learning to identify and express your feelings will be a great gift to your children.

Sadness, loneliness, love, compassion, empathy, and understanding are feelings that come from your heart. Honesty, fear, anger, and courage are feelings that come from your gut. When it comes to communicating, not one of these is the all-time solution. There are times when judgment and analysis from your head will serve best. Other circumstances call for listening to the love, compassion, or sadness of your heart. Still other times require you to be gut-level honest or to listen to your fears, anger, or courage. The solution to many communication problems is to find the appropriate balance.

After Joyce's divorce, she realized that a big chasm had developed between her and her daughter, Julia. When Joyce learned the skills of communicating from her head, heart, or gut, she was able to bridge that chasm. She shared the following excerpt from her journal:

> *About six months ago, Julia took me to a movie. Before the movie, we were talking, and I started to listen to what she was saying instead of arguing.*
>
> *I didn't realize I hadn't been listening until I started to listen. I could see how, in the past, I would go right to my head and would try to explain my point of view instead of listening to her from my heart.*
>
> *It took self-discipline to bite my tongue. When the conversation ended, I had this uneasy feeling that nothing had been solved. I hadn't done any of my usual behaviors, like giving her advice or telling her*

*the "correct way" (my way) to see things. However, over the weeks I noticed our relationship got better, even though there was still some uneasiness.*

*About a month after this first "listening" experience, I drove her home after a family dinner. She made it a point that she wanted me to drive her home. I could tell she wanted to say something to me, but she was nervous. So I decided to share with her from my heart. I said, "I feel so bad about the gap in our relationship. We have this kind of superficial relationship. I love you, and I think you love me, and when we spend time together it's very pleasant and cordial, but it feels so superficial. I just wish there was something we could do to close the gap."*

*Julia said, "I'm not going to talk about this anymore. I've been through a lot. I'm not getting into this stuff again."*

*I kept saying, "I think I'm a better listener now. I've learned a lot. I used to think I knew how to listen, but I didn't. Please give me another try. I want to know what you've gone through."*

*So Julia started talking to me. It was very painful to hear what she had to say. It was just breaking my heart to really listen to her, because she told me that she felt that the person who had always helped her deal with her pain had abandoned her (during the divorce) when she was in the most pain of her life. She wondered how I could really love her and do that. She realized that many of the things she had believed were just myths—that her mother was just a person but not the person Julia believed her to be.*

*Julia said, "In a way, I have to thank you because I'm a better person for going through this, because I was just going along in life and having a good time. All I thought about was where the next party was. I didn't really take anything seriously. I figured life was just a game. When this happened, I found out differently. Life is very serious, and I'm the one in control of my life. Because of that, I made a lot of decisions about not abusing drugs, about how I'm going to spend my time, about what's important to me, how important school is to me. I don't think our relationship is really bad, but it can never be the same now because you're different than I thought you were. You were my mother and now you're this person."*

*I was sitting there crying hard because I really heard Julia with my heart. My heart was breaking, and I kept saying, "I'm just so sorry that you had to go through this. I'm so sorry I couldn't listen to you. I heard everything you said as a criticism—I couldn't hear what was behind it. I was too defensive. I can imagine how invalidating that must have been. How insulting that must have been to you! You know, I love you so much, and it's so hard for me to see you go through pain. And to think that you went through all this! I just wish I would've known. I wish I would've understood. I wish I could have! You thought you saw me being happy, but I was going through incredible pain. You didn't see the pain; you saw something else. And someday, when you're ready, I'd like to tell you about what was going on for me then. I don't think this would be a very good time, but there's a lot you don't know and a lot you don't understand. I hope someday you'll want to know."*

*This was all happening in the car, in the driveway. The two of us were just sobbing, and I was holding her, and I said, "I just love you so much, and I feel so bad."*

*She said, "And I love you."*

*That big barrier got broken down between us. It was painful to listen from my heart, but it was worth it. I feel like I have my daughter back.*

## COMMUNICATE GUT FEELINGS

The custom of our society is to discount or ignore feelings, or worse yet, to medicate them away—especially those from the gut. You've been taught not to feel angry and not to be honest if telling the truth might hurt someone else's feelings. (Isn't that an interesting paradox? It must be okay for other people to have feelings because you aren't supposed to hurt them, but you are supposed to suppress feelings of your own.) Although a great deal of lip service is given to developing as an individual, you are judged when you don't conform to the norm. How often have you tried to tell someone how you really feel and they respond with advice or discount your feelings or suggest you should see your doctor who has the perfect pill to make them go away?

If you don't learn to acknowledge your feelings, to listen to what they have to teach you, and to express them in ways that are respectful to yourself and others, your life will be superficial, without substance. If you are able to do these things for yourself, you will then be able to teach them to your children.

Part of your job as a kind and firm parent is to help your kids acknowledge and understand their feelings, be comfortable with expressing feelings in a respectful manner, express feelings as information and not as absolutes, and help them stand up for themselves.

Teenagers need to know that it's okay to have feelings, no matter what they are, and that they don't have to do anything about them. Feeling is not the same as doing. Having what many people consider to be "bad" feelings (anger, jealousy, hopelessness) does not make someone a bad person; everyone has these feelings. Actually, there aren't good or bad feelings, there are just feelings. No matter how intense those feelings are, they won't kill you, especially if you express them respectfully. The more you do this, you'll notice that these feelings come, and then they go instead of festering inside you.

You teach your kids about communicating gut feelings when you hear their feelings and validate them and when you share your own feelings using the listening skills taught in this chapter. When you don't help your kids express their feelings, they are often labeled as "depressed."

## THE HAIRBALL OF DEPRESSION

We're sure you've heard and used the term "depression" to describe a myriad of symptoms and issues in your life and the lives of those you know and love. It's a convenient catchall phrase that covers a lot of ground and often results in a diagnosis from a medical person accompanied by a prescription for antidepressants or antianxiety medication or both. We suggest that instead of using this term, you think of what is going on as a "hairball of feelings" that needs to be pulled apart so that progress can be made toward encouragement. When you say someone is depressed, it sounds like that person has a medical condition that is sad, dangerous, and overwhelming. If instead you separate out the feelings, you'll discover the discouragement behind the feelings that will give you information about how to encourage that can lead to immediate improvement.

Jules, a high school junior, was often "diagnosed" as depressed by his friends, family, and even at times, by himself. His dad was learning about feelings in his parenting class and brought home a chart of feeling faces. He wondered if it would help Jules to cough up his hairball of feelings, so he showed him the chart from his class and said, "Jules, I'm learning about feelings in my parenting class. Since the only feeling words I know are 'hungry,' 'angry,' and 'tired,' I've been using this chart to learn more feeling words. I wonder if you are feeling any of the feelings on this chart."

Dad realized that Jules needed help identifying feelings as much as he did, as neither of them had much of a feeling-words vocabulary. When Jules looked at the feeling faces (page 97), he quickly picked out several. He told his dad he was lonely because he didn't have a lot of friends; he was disappointed because he thought his grades would be better and that he'd be in line for any college of his choice; he was embarrassed because he didn't have a date for homecoming; and he was angry because his parents took away his computer and Wii privileges because of poor grades. On top of that, he was scared because he thought he had what the TV ads called "a chemical imbalance."

Dad was feeling overwhelmed hearing all this, but also relieved, realizing that maybe he and Jules could tackle some of these issues one by one. Dad also suspected that Jules was smoking dope daily and partying on weekends, something he had done as a teen to take the edge off his own feelings. He wanted to find a way to continue the discussion with his son, so he asked, "Jules, would you be willing to keep talking about feelings with me every now and then? I think it would help us both."

"Does this mean I'm going to get my computer back?" Jules asked, with a grin on his face.

"Who knows, son. I'm already having a better understanding of what is going on, and I'm open to learning more. If we can take our time figuring out this feeling stuff, maybe we can even find other ways to deal with your schoolwork."

If your kid is like Jules, when you worry about "depression," ask your teen to talk about his or her feelings. Listen without judging. Don't label your teen. If you think the issues are beyond your comfort zone, look for help from a counselor/therapist who understands that throwing drugs at the situation isn't the answer.

## HONESTY: A TOOL FOR DEVELOPING A FEELING-WORDS VOCABULARY

Being honest with your teen about how you feel now and about how you felt and what you did as a teenager is extremely valuable. Often parents are afraid to talk about what they did as kids because they think their kids will take it as encouragement to do the same things. But many teenagers have told us the opposite is true. Don't be afraid to be honest with your teen—it's an excellent way to encourage communication.

When her fourteen-year-old daughter, Erin, began going steady, Linda decided to be honest with her. She said to Erin, "I want to share some things that happened to me as a teenager . . . but I have to tell you, it's scary for me! I did some things that weren't good for me, and some things I knew my parents wouldn't like one bit—and I'm scared that if you know I did these things, you'll want to do them, too. But I'm not going to pay attention to my fears, because I think what I tell you can be helpful."

Linda took a deep breath:

*I was sexually active from the time I was in the tenth grade. I was very lucky that I didn't get pregnant. I was having sex because I was looking for love . . . I didn't know that wasn't the way to find it. I thought my boyfriends wouldn't like me if I didn't do what they wanted. I didn't have enough self-love and self-confidence to think about what I wanted.*

*It was also a real moral issue for me, because I was taught that it was a sin to engage in sex before marriage. So I felt like a sinner, I felt guilty, and then I did it anyway—which made me feel even worse. I could never bring myself to ask anyone for information or ask about birth control. In fact, I kept promising myself I'd never do it again, but then I would. Then I'd feel guilty all over again.*

*I wonder what I would've done if I'd felt loved, . . . if I had information and even permission to use birth control, . . . if I knew I'd be accepted no matter what choices I made. I have a hunch I might've been much wiser in my decisions. I don't know if I would have abstained, but the chances are much greater that I would have in most cases—the times when I was more worried about being rejected than about what was right for me. That's why I want to tell you what I wish my parents could have told me.*

*I get scared that you'll get involved in sex before you've developed enough judgment to understand long-term results like pregnancy, your reputation, and disease. I wonder if you respect yourself enough to feel good about saying no if you want to, rather than feeling like you have to give in to someone else's demands. I wish I could protect you from being hurt by any mistakes you might make, but I know you have to make your own mistakes and learn whatever you learn from living your life the way you choose. Just know that I'll always be here to love you and accept you unconditionally, and I'll be glad to give you information if you ever want it.*

Linda used a lot of words—which is okay when you're sharing feelings from the heart and gut. (Eye rolling from your kids is rare when you share this way.) She was touched by how effective her sharing was. Erin told her all about the kids at school who everyone knew were "doing it." Erin told her mother that she didn't have any trouble saying no because she'd noticed how it wasn't long before everyone in school knew "everything;" she didn't want people to talk about her that way.

Linda would not have known what was going on with Erin if she hadn't decided to be honest with her. Aware that Erin might change her mind about sex as she grows older, Linda planned to keep the lines of communication open so Erin could feel free to use her mother as a resource anytime.

It takes honesty and courage to get in touch with your own feelings, the source of those feelings, and what you want to do about them. When communicating honestly about feelings, it's easy to get sidetracked into explanations, rationalizations, attacks, defensiveness, and other reactions. Following the "I feel" formula (I feel _____ because _____ and I wish _____ ) helps keep you centered on your feelings, the reasons for your feelings, and possible solutions. Notice the word "possible." Asking for what you wish doesn't mean anyone else has the responsibility to give it to you. Neither should you expect anyone else to agree with you or feel the same. Instead, the "I feel" formula is an effective procedure for honoring, respecting, and expressing yourself in a way that's respectful to others. (Use the feeling-faces chart on the opposite page to help you identify your feelings.)

## THE "I FEEL" FORMULA

Note how the italicized words are used in the variations of the "I feel" formula that follow.

"I *feel* upset about the dishes not being done *because* I like looking at a clean kitchen and cooking in a clean kitchen—and I *wish* you'd do them before I start cooking."

"I feel hurt when you put me down, and I wish you wouldn't do that." In this case, the *because it hurts my feelings* was omitted since it's clearly understood. The formula is flexible; it provides guidelines, not rules. When appropriate, it's helpful to include *because* and *I wish* because they help you stay in touch with the whole picture and give others as much information as possible.

"I feel happy for you for getting that A on your report card because I know how hard you worked for it." This comment ends with the focus where it belongs—on the effort rather than the person. To say "I'm so proud of you for getting an A" leaves your kids feeling as though you won't be so proud of them if they don't get A's. Your children need to feel that you're proud of them no matter what.

"I feel upset about that F on your report card because I'm afraid you might be missing out on something that could benefit you. I wish you'd take another look at what a good education could mean to you." Rather than attacking character, comments like this invite your teens to look at how their behavior affects their lives.

"I feel really angry when you hit your brother because I dislike violence. I'd like you to consider other ways to express your feelings and other ways to get what you want." This comment models for your child that it's okay to feel angry but not okay to be abusive to others. It also allows room for follow-up on the issue of violence, which could be discussed at a family meeting or at another time when both parent and child are in good moods. At that time, a list could be made of possible nonviolent ways of dealing with anger and for getting what you want.

## THE "YOU FEEL" FORMULA

In rare instances when your kids do open up to you and try to express their feelings (sometimes in disrespectful ways), you may react negatively (with a disrespectful response). If you tell your child he shouldn't feel that way or he should be more respectful, or if you counterattack him in any way, don't be surprised when he grows up with the idea that it's not okay to have feelings or that he should suppress them.

When you model the "I feel" formula, you help children learn how to honor and express their feelings in respectful ways. It helps to validate *their feelings* with the "you feel" formula. Sometimes it's easy to validate what they've said because it's very clear. In these instances, it's important that you don't sound like a parrot. Your intent—to hear what your teen is saying—will come through if you validate the feelings behind the words instead of simply repeating the words.

DJ was watching television when his father came into the room and asked him to take out the garbage. DJ ignored Dad. Five minutes later, Dad came back into the room and said, "Turn off that TV right now and take out the garbage."

DJ said, "How come I have to do everything you want right now? How would you like it if I told you to turn off the TV and do something for me right now?"

Dad could see that he'd created resistance and defensiveness with his demand. Fortunately, he remembered the "you feel" formula.

> DAD: You hate it when I tell you to do something right now and you feel angry because I'm not being respectful of your time and interests. Do you wish I'd give you more warning or more choices about when it would be convenient for you?
>
> DJ: Yeah.
>
> DAD: You're right. I was disrespectful. When would you be willing to empty the garbage?
>
> DJ: At the next commercial.
>
> DAD: Good enough for me.

When this dad shared the preceding example with his parent study group, he added, "Before, I would've escalated the problem by telling my son not to get smart with me instead of realizing I had been disrespectful to him."

A mother in the same group shared:

> *When my daughter used to tell me about her fights with her friends I would say, "Oh, honey, I'm sure it'll be okay tomorrow. You know you always have these fights, and they don't last long." She would stomp off to her bedroom and slam the door. Now, I say something like, "You feel really bad when you have had a fight with your friend because you aren't sure you'll be able to make up, and then you won't have a best friend." I see the relief in her face from feeling listened to and understood. Then she says, "Yes, but I'm sure we'll make up tomorrow." Instead of trying to fix problems or make them go away, it's actually much easier to reflect feelings with understanding. It's also comforting to know that she now feels validated rather than put down.*

## REFLECTING YOUR TEEN'S FEELINGS IS NOT ALWAYS EASY

Sometimes your teen's feelings are not clear. This means listening with a "third ear" to what might be underneath an outburst and reflecting to them what you've heard. Your reflection may not be accurate, but if you present it in a friendly manner, with real intent to understand, your teens will help you out by correcting your perception.

After reading about the "you feel" formula, Nina thought she'd give it a try with her fifteen-year-old son, Jayden. She thought back to her conversation with him during lunch. It hadn't gone well. Jayden had announced that he was no longer going to take piano lessons and that if she didn't like it, too bad. If she tried to force him, he'd go to the lesson, but he'd refuse to practice. He told her that out of nine years of lessons, he had enjoyed one of them and had done the other eight years for her. Now he was going to take up the guitar and she couldn't stop him.

Nina gave her usual ineffective lecture, this time telling Jayden that if he stopped, he'd never be able to get back to where he was with the piano. She had hoped that the lecture would get Jayden to change his mind, which it didn't, and really never had.

Nina wondered what it would mean to listen with a "third ear." She decided to try again, using the "you feel" formula. She asked Jayden if they could talk about the piano once more, and Jayden said, "I haven't changed my mind, so I don't see the point."

Nina said, "I feel bad that I didn't listen to you and that I just gave one of my lectures. I'd like to try again so I can understand more about your thinking. You were saying you've been taking piano lessons for me for eight years. You must feel angry about that."

Jayden said, "Mom, I'm not angry, but I'm ready to move on. I like the guitar and I think it will be easy for me to play it with my music background. I'm going to put a band together and if I can pick up guitar, I could play that in the band."

Nina took a deep breath, resisted the urge to lecture, and said, "You feel excited about moving on and you're looking forward to getting a band together. I can understand that. I agree that it should be a lot easier to learn the next instrument with your background."

Jayden looked shocked. He wasn't used to his mom agreeing with him. He was waiting for the lecture, but when it didn't come, he added, "Mom, I've given this a lot of thought. I'm not a little kid anymore, and I know what I like."

"Honey," Mom said, "I know you're very thoughtful and know your own mind. If you'd like my help finding a guitar teacher, I'd be happy to do that."

"Thanks, Mom, but I think I can pick up what I need on my own, and if I can't, I'll let you know. I've been watching some YouTube videos that are really helpful. You can save your money on lessons. But I would love it if you'd help pay for a guitar."

"Let me give that some thought. Have you thought about renting one for a while till you see if you really like it enough to buy one?"

Jayden's mom realized that she could communicate better when she listened with a "third ear," but it was going to take some time to get used to giving up her influence on what Jayden did. Who said it's easy to parent a teen? The methods we teach will help you bridge the gap between your child's dependence on you and his budding desire for independence from you. You won't always get what you want, but you just might get the joy of knowing you are helping your kid move on in a healthy way.

## LEARNING THE LANGUAGE OF POWERFUL COMMUNICATION

Keep remembering that teens are struggling with ways to feel powerful. Being powerful is a good quality, as long as it is accompanied with respect and responsibility. As you learn how to communicate using the language of powerful communication, you'll be able to help your teen feel powerful without ending up in power struggles. Because parents have asked us, "But what do I say? Give me the words," we provide the following phrases to help you communicate to your teens that they are powerful. Saying this does not imply that teens have power over you; it simply means that they are powerful and can impact their world.

### POWERFUL COMMUNICATIONS: WORDS FOR PARENTS

*Let's make a deal! How about you help your brother sweep the patio and I'll drive you to the movie.*

*Let's negotiate. Why don't you tell me what you have in mind for Friday night and then I'll tell you what I have in mind, and we'll see if we can find something we both can live with.*

*Here's the way it works. First we go through your closet and then go over your clothing budget and then we go shopping.*

*Would you be willing to work with me on figuring out whether you want to improve your math grade, and if so, how you could go about that?*

*Why don't we both take a break, cool off, and then come back and try again.*

*In our house we agreed to solve problems at our family meeting. Instead of arguing, one of us can write it on the list for our next meeting.*

*Tuesday is your brother's day for the washer and dryer. Do you remember which day is yours?*

*Time for our break from media.*

*When you have picked up the dog poop, then I'll be happy to watch your YouTube skateboarding video.*

*That's one way. I look at it differently. Want to hear what I think?*

*We can listen to each other without agreeing.*

*We'll do it this way until we have time to work out a plan we all like.*

*Let's start with a set curfew and change it as we need to. We can put it on the agenda for the family meeting.*

*Let's try this out for a day, week, month, and then reevaluate.*

*You may drive our car, borrow my clothes, et cetera, as long as you return them clean; otherwise, I'll have to say no until I feel like trying again.*

Compare the preceding statements with your normal communication, which usually sounds more like, "Because I said so," or "When you have a home of your own, you can do what you want, and not until then," or "Do this and do that!" Quite a difference!

## QUICK TIPS FOR COMMUNICATION

There are many facets to communicating effectively. The following tips will serve as additional guidelines to help you keep a respectful relationship with your teen. Since these tips are so important, we give both short samples and longer explanations of each.

1. **Avoid the blame game:** "I'm not interested in who started this. I'd like to know how you girls can work this out without physical violence."
2. **Keep it simple:** "What was your understanding of our agreement about refueling the car?"
3. **Use only one word:** "Dishes!"
4. **Use ten words or fewer:** "Bring dirty dishes from your room, please."
5. **Avoid words:** Parent points to broom and floor while smiling until kid gets up and sweeps as promised.
6. **Get permission before giving advice:** "May I share something with you that I think might help?"
7. **Let your teens have the last word:** " . . . . . . . . . !"
8. **Hang out:** Just sit in the same room as your kid flipping through the paper or a magazine. You'll be surprised how this often opens up communication you might otherwise have not gotten.

## ACTING INSTEAD OF REACTING

We often caution about acting instead of reacting. Back talk is a challenge that often invites reacting. Communicating is more than just what you say. It is about how it is received. As you read the difference between reacting and acting to back talk, imagine what teens might be thinking, feeling, and deciding if they were hearing these comments.

### REACTING PARENT
1. "Don't talk to me that way, young lady!"
2. "Go to your room and don't come out until you can be respectful!"
3. "You are grounded for a week!"
4. "How can you talk to me that way after all I have done for you?"
5. "You just lost all your privileges."

6. "Maybe military school will teach you to be more respectful of authority."

7. "No child of mine is going to talk like that."

8. "You will be respectful if I have to beat it into you."

## ACTING PARENT

1. "Hmmm. I wonder what I did to upset you so much?"

2. "Wow! You are really angry."

3. "I need to take some time out until we can treat each other respectfully."

4. "I need a hug. Please come find me when you are ready for one."

5. "What would help us right now—some time out or putting this problem on the family-meeting agenda?"

6. Don't say anything. Give energetic support—which means to give out love energetically—a loving look and/or your hand over your heart.

7. Listen with your lips closed, while saying, "Hmmm. Umhmmm."

8. "Do you know that I really love you?"

In this chapter you have learned many skills to ensure that your teens will hear what you have to say—because you have learned to hear what they say. Look at the barriers to communication and find the ones you use most. Work at catching and stopping yourself from using them, even if it's midstream. Practicing healthy communication skills will greatly enhance your relationship with your teens.

## KIND AND FIRM PARENTING TOOLS TO REMEMBER

1. Review what teens have to say about how to improve communications and use as many methods as you can with your teen.

2. Ask "Anything else?" until your teen stops talking, to really open your eyes to your teen's separate reality.

3. Feelings aren't good or bad and you won't die from them, so work on developing a feeling-words vocabulary to help you and yours express your feelings respectfully.

4. Although you may have grown up trying to be tactful and worrying about hurting others' feelings, you can probably communicate with much more honesty and still not offend anyone. In fact, you might even feel closer to others.

5. Of all the communication help in this chapter, the "I feel" and "you feel" formulas help the most when you learn how to use them with real feeling words.

6. Teens communicate better when you really listen to them and when you include them in discussions about issues that affect them.

7. The language of powerful communication can help you avoid power struggles, so put the list where you can easily access it.

8. Using fewer words, hanging out, and asking permission go a long way to make the communication you do have with your teen more effective.

*Practical Application Activity*

## THE "I FEEL" PROCESS

1. Reread the pages in this chapter on the "I feel" and "You feel" processes.

2. Refer to the feeling-faces chart on page 97.

3. Think of a situation in which, no matter how many times you tried to communicate something to your teen, you couldn't get anywhere. Look at the chart on page 97 and find the feeling face and feeling word that best fits how you felt in that circumstance.

4. Write a sentence using the "I feel _____ because _____ and I wish _____" formula, making sure you use the feeling word from the chart after the word "feel." Read your sentence to your teen and see what kind of result you get.

# 7

# DO FAMILY MEETINGS WORK
# WITH TEENAGERS?

## A PARENTING TOOL THAT TEACHES SO MUCH
## OF WHAT YOU WANT FOR YOUR TEENS

F amily meetings are one of the most important parenting tools you
can use during the teen years—*and* you may experience resistance
from your teens.

Mary and Mark enjoyed family meetings with their mom and dad
from the time they were four and seven until they became teenagers.
Then they started to complain about how stupid family meetings were.
Mom and Dad negotiated some give-and-take. "Humor us about continuing our weekly tradition of having family meetings and we'll agree
to shorten them to fifteen minutes instead of thirty." The funny part
of this story is that Mary, one of the most verbal complainers, spent

the night with her friend. The next morning she announced, "That family is so screwed up. They should be having family meetings." Don't take the ranting and raving of your teens personally, and continue to use the parenting skills that serve your teens—even when they complain.

The family meeting is a valuable tool because it provides a platform for creating and maintaining dignity and respect while teaching teens valuable social and life skills. During family meetings kids and parents practice:

- Listening skills.

- Brainstorming skills.

- Problem-solving skills.

- Mutual respect.

- The value of cooling off before solving a problem. (Problems are put on the family meeting agenda so a cooling-off period takes place before focusing on solutions to the challenge.)

- Concern for others.

- Cooperation.

- Accountability in a safe environment. (People don't worry about admitting mistakes when they know they will be supported to find solutions instead of experiencing blame, shame, or pain.)

- How to choose solutions that are respectful to everyone concerned.

- Social interest (contribution).

- How to avoid power struggles by respectfully sharing control and responsibility.

- Learning that mistakes are wonderful opportunities to grow.

- Giving everyone a chance to feel a sense of belonging and significance.

- Having fun as a family.

Family meetings provide an opportunity for parents to do the following:

- Avoid micromanaging children, so children learn self-discipline.

- Listen in ways that invite children to listen.

- Create good memories through a family tradition.

- Model all of the skills they want their children to learn.

Family meetings can be as important to families as regular staff meetings are to any well-run business. During family meetings, you can help your teens build character as you all explore feelings, discover separate realities, and work together to find solutions to family problems. Your teens will learn to "look for the good" by giving and receiving compliments.

Family meetings are a great way to communicate with teens because there is a cooling-off period before you discuss most issues. Some people say that teens don't like family meetings, but our experience is that teens don't like being lectured to, criticized, or bossed. If that is what happens at your family meetings, your teens won't want to attend. Remember, teens often come with an "attitude," so don't be put off by their style if they appear to be less than enthusiastic.

There is never just one way to do a family meeting. Some families prefer a more formal approach and some a more casual approach. You can decide what works for you—as long as meetings are scheduled regularly once a week.

At your family meeting rotate the job of chairperson and recorder (if you have one), use an agenda to which anyone may add items during the week, and seek consensus or temporary interim decisions. Include compliments and appreciations at the start of each meeting to stress the idea that working together means identifying the positive aspects of family life and not simply focusing on problems. As each issue on the agenda comes up, check to see if it is still an issue. If it is, take turns talking about it by going around the table twice for each person to make comments or suggestions. If it's hard for family members to take turns, you might find the addition of a talking stick helpful. (Whoever has the talking stick is the one whose turn it is to talk.) For items that need more discussion, table them till the following meeting.

## USE FAMILY MEETINGS TO INCREASE UNDERSTANDING OF SEPARATE REALITIES

At family meetings, some issues may not get solved; they may simply be discussed. That's okay. Because teens, and even spouses, often have completely different realities, it is important to have a time when everyone in the family can speak and be listened to with respect. Remember that listening doesn't mean agreeing; it simply means learning more about each family member's thoughts.

In the O'Brien family, Dad felt that everyone should sit down together for their meals. He came from a family where everyone ate three meals together. He felt that this was how it should be—that this was how a family shows love—and that he felt loved when people sat down and ate with him.

In Mom's family growing up, her father was working in other towns most of the time. Her own mother gave up trying to deal with fussy appetites and allowed the kids to fix their own food, except on Sundays when they would have a roast or chicken dinner. Therefore, Mom felt that mealtimes didn't matter, except for special occasions. However, she also had a vague feeling that this was not how it "should" be done.

The two teenagers in this family, David and Cindy, were more interested in doing their own thing than sitting together for family meals. Dad, feeling like the odd man out, decided he wanted to discuss his concern about mealtimes at a family meeting.

DAD: I feel really disappointed that I can't get more cooperation for something as simple as getting the family to have at least two meals together a week. (Dad's tone of voice expressed judgments rather than feelings.)

DAVID [defensively]: Ah, you get more than two meals a week.

CINDY: Yeah, Dad.

MOM: I'd like to know why this is so important to Dad.

DAVID: I know why.

MOM: Let's see if you can give three reasons why.

DAVID: He wants to spend more time with his family.

DAD: Yes.

DAVID: Because he loves us.

DAD: Yes.

CINDY: Because he wants us to learn manners!

DAD: No. I want you to sit with me because I want to know you love me.

CINDY: Oh, you know we love you.

DAD: How would I know that?

The family has stopped going around the table taking turns, but they are still discussing Dad's issue and making some progress on understanding, which is more important than sticking to the agreement of going around the table twice.

MOM: What does eating together have to do with feeling loved?

DAD: Because when I grew up, my family did that three times a day. That's why I got the idea that people who love each other do that. I thought it would be that way with my wife and kids.

MOM: David, what does mealtime mean to you?

DAVID: A time to get fed.

CINDY: I just hate it that when we're done eating, we have to just sit there!

MOM: It doesn't matter to me. My mother gave up on mealtimes. We all fixed what we wanted, except on Sundays.

DAD: Is there any way to work this out so we can all get our needs met?

DAVID: I have a comment. I think we do eat together a lot.

MOM: So you think that you eat with us more than we think you do?

DAVID: Yes.

DAD: I think a normal mealtime in our house is just me.

DAVID: You're exaggerating.

CINDY: I get so hungry because I don't eat breakfast or lunch, so I come home and eat something, and you have a cow!

MOM: If you want the kids to eat with you, could you give up harping about what they eat? You have so many rules about how it should be—what we should eat, how long we should sit there, and on and on.

DAD: I can see that I've done that. It just didn't occur to me that other people felt so differently about mealtime than I did. I'm willing to stop harping about what you eat, and I won't make you stay at the table when you are through. Under those circumstances, how many times would you be willing to sit down and eat with me?

DAVID: I wouldn't mind starting dinner most of the time together, at least four times a week, if you wouldn't put us down so much.

CINDY: That sounds good to me.

MOM: I'm certainly willing to be more considerate about what's important to you. I just didn't know it was that important.

DAD: That sounds reasonable to me. So when will we have our next meal together?

MOM: How about tomorrow night?

DAVID: I'll be there.

CINDY: Me, too.

This family might have continued bickering for years if they hadn't learned to listen to each other's feelings. They continued to have family meetings in which they heard each other's feelings and perceptions and then worked on solutions that were respectful to everyone. You can create this kind of openness and respect at your house by focusing on listening and curiosity.

Your family will run more smoothly when you hold weekly family meetings. During these meetings, in addition to sharing mutual appreciations and focusing on solutions to challenges that are put on the agenda, you can plan menus, calendars, shopping trips, outings, and other joint activities. If you are like most families, you will need to discuss guidelines for the use of televisions, computers and other electronic devices, and phones. Family meetings are an excellent time to give out allowances, especially if that is something that would work better when scheduled regularly.

### GUIDELINES FOR EFFECTIVE FAMILY MEETINGS

1. Set a time line for the meeting. Some families spend ten to fifteen minutes a week while others meet for a half hour or more. Use a timer and, if needed, a designated timekeeper. (Teens are more comfortable when they know when the meeting will end.)
2. Start with compliments and/or appreciations.
3. Prioritize items on the agenda by asking if there are any items that can be eliminated because they have already been handled or if any need top priority.
4. Discuss each item and let everyone voice his or her opinion without comments or criticism from others. Many families find that going around the table twice serves as a safe way to discuss items without one family member monopolizing or others not being heard.
5. If the problem calls for more than a discussion, which is more often than not, brainstorm for solutions.
6. Choose one solution that everyone can live with (consensus) and try it for a week.
7. Table difficult issues to discuss at the next regularly scheduled family meeting when there has been more time for calming down.

The more you adhere to the preceding guidelines, the better your meetings will go. This doesn't mean that every meeting will be a huge success, but over time, you'll have increased cooperation and respect in your family. If you are having problems, remember that it takes time for everyone to practice and learn the skills necessary for effective family meetings. Have patience and keep practicing. When families aren't used to working this way, it takes time and patience to be efficient and effective—but it's worth the effort. You might also see if any of the following hints would improve your family meetings.

## HINTS FOR IMPROVING FAMILY MEETINGS

1. Hold family meetings at the same time each week, not only when there's a crisis.
2. Although family meetings with older kids can be quite rewarding, they can also be difficult to arrange because of busy schedules. One family solved the problem by setting the next meeting date at the end of each meeting. (Interestingly, the meeting was always set for the same day of the week, but the teen liked having the choice.)
3. Working together takes time and practice, but the goal is progress not perfection. All family members must have the opportunity to be present. Some family members may refuse to come, and younger children may get restless and leave in the middle.
4. Be sure that kids feel they're taken seriously and treated as important, contributing members of their family.
5. When someone shares at a family meeting, everyone else should listen respectfully, without arguing or correcting.
6. Have family members take turns running the meeting or making notes of the decisions.
7. When working on solutions for agenda items, consensus is a key ingredient for success. If everyone doesn't agree on a decision, dissenters will probably undermine any progress that could be made.

8. Talking about controversial subjects without trying to decide on a solution is often helpful. For extremely controversial issues, it may take several meetings to reach any kind of consensus.

9. It's okay if your family can't reach agreement. Live with the results of indecision, which usually means keeping things the way they've been or doing as the parents say until the issue can be worked out at a future meeting.

10. Parents should make sure they don't monopolize. Lecturing or giving orders defeats the purpose of family meetings.

11. Focus on items that are less controversial, such as time for fun, allowances, and so on, until kids believe their input is wanted and respected.

It's often obvious to us that families could solve many of their problems themselves through family meetings. But too many families don't spend enough time together. Instead, parents leave lists of orders for the kids—which the kids resist doing. And the kids can never find a good time to ask their parents for help, so they become demanding instead. Some family members do more than their share of work, and then, feeling resentful, they nag and punish other family members for being lazy.

Although it may seem more efficient to issue orders and plan for your teens without their input, it's less effective than the long-term parenting that teaches your children life skills. Bryce and Barbara's story in the next section provides an excellent example.

## WHAT DOES A REAL FAMILY MEETING LOOK LIKE AND SOUND LIKE?

Bryce and Barbara had been married for five years. Like many stepfamilies, their lives were extremely busy because both parents worked, so they handled everything on the fly. Bryce's daughter from his first marriage lived with them on weekends, holidays, and summers. Therefore, whatever schedule they established changed at least once a week. They decided to hold family meetings as a way to reduce confusion and chaos. Everyone was present: Barbara's two kids from her first marriage, seventeen-year-old Todd and fourteen-year-old Laurie, and Bryce's daughter, fourteen-year-old Ann. They were able to solve a problem that they thought was unsolvable.

> BRYCE: I'd like to start our meeting with appreciations. I'd like to let Todd know I appreciate that he cleaned the garage yesterday. Ann, I want you to know I appreciate you leaving your boyfriend behind so you could spend the summer with us.
>
> ANN: I'd like to thank Todd for offering to drive me to the mall today. I appreciate Mom for taking me miniature golfing.
>
> TODD: I'd like to thank Mom for letting me sleep in the last few days.
>
> BARBARA: I'd like to thank Dad for cooking dinner last night.
>
> LAURIE: I'd like to pass.

(Imagine, just for a minute, how people in your family would feel giving and receiving appreciations. It is so seldom that people take the time to say something nice to one another. We are sure you and your family would enjoy meetings if only for the positive reinforcements.)

> TODD: I'd like to start with Laurie's complaint, since that seems like the most important.
>
> LAURIE: I don't think it's fair just because I'm the only girl in the family that I have to share my room when Ann comes. I like Ann, but nobody even asks me if it's okay. Ann gets up earlier than I do, and she makes so much noise that I can't sleep. And I don't like listening to Ann's music all the time.
>
> BARBARA: I'm sorry, Laurie. I had no idea you felt this way. You're right, we just assume Ann will stay with you, and

we never ask. I can't imagine where Ann would stay if she weren't welcome in your room.

BRYCE: Laurie, if you had more choice and could work out the wake-up time and the music with Ann, would it be okay for her to stay with you?

ANN: I could use my earphones when I listen to my music. I'll try to be quiet in the morning. Maybe I could leave my clothes in the bathroom and get ready in there.

LAURIE: Now I feel like a real brat. (She starts to cry.)

BARBARA: Laurie, I'm glad we have a place where we can say how we really feel about things, and I'm glad you had the courage to tell us how upset you were. We weren't being considerate of you, and we didn't realize it. Now we do. I know we can work this out.

BRYCE: I've been thinking of moving my home office to the main office downtown. If I did that, it would give us another room. In the meantime, Ann could use the foldaway bed.

LAURIE: I want Ann to stay with me! I just wanted to be asked. And Ann, you can get ready in our room in the morning; you're not really that noisy. But I would like it if you'd use your earphones when you listen to the stereo.

ANN: Thanks, Laurie. I'd much rather share a room with you than be alone in Dad's office.

The rest of the family meeting was spent trying to find a time everyone could be together for the next meeting—not an easy task in most busy families!

## USE FAMILY MEETINGS TO ESTABLISH COOPERATION (INCLUDING CHORES)

Relatively speaking, teenagers will be more motivated to participate in household chores if they have been involved in working on a plan. We say "relatively speaking" because, again, chores are the parents' priority, not the kids'. As a parent, your task is not to make your teens like doing chores, but to gain as much cooperation as possible.

One way to improve the chore situation at your house is to invite the family to make a list of household chores that need to be done. Next to each item, the recorder notes the family consensus on how often that particular chore needs to be done and what the deadline should be for getting it done. Finally, family members pick which chores they would be willing to do that week. Some of the more unpopular chores, such as cleaning toilets, may have to be placed in a hat for some lucky person to draw. It's good to have one person monitor the chore list each day to see whether chores have been completed by the deadline. If a chore doesn't get done, the monitor finds the responsible person, lets him or her know about the missed deadline, and reinforces that it's time to do the chore. Parents should avoid monitoring since it sounds like nagging. In many families, the youngest child likes this job and does it very well.

When families use this kind of chore routine, they find that deadlines work best if they are set for times when people are most likely to be around the house, such as first thing in the morning, after school or work, before dinner, or before bedtime. Follow-through (as discussed in Chapter 5) is effective for holding people accountable for their agreements.

Some families find that cooperation about chores increases when everyone works together. Perhaps it's that old "Misery loves company," but setting aside an hour a week for housework when everyone is present to work together usually succeeds better than hoping things will get done at different times during the week. Of course, there are also the daily chores that can't wait, but even those go better when families have a chore time when everyone is doing something to help the family.

Some families are deeply involved in power struggles around chores. When this is the case, it may take smaller steps at a family meeting to progress toward cooperation, such as asking each family member what one chore he or she would be willing to do daily until the next family meeting. The idea is to try something for a week and at the next meeting discuss and evaluate what everyone learned. We know this is a slow process, but building family involvement when discord has been the norm often starts slowly and then snowballs into something wonderful.

Kathy H shared the following on the Positive Discipline Social Network (www.positivediscipline.ning.com) in the PD for Teens group.

*We had our first family meeting yesterday. Yay!!!! I was pleasantly surprised at how well it went. At first my 15-year-old girl and 11-year-old boy were quite resistant to sitting down and talking. I am guessing they thought a lecture was next up on the "agenda." I opened with compliments which neither one is ready to give just yet so I gave my compliments. Then we talked about our issue from earlier that morning about who rides up front in the car. I asked them what would be a solution that they could both live with and miraculously they came up with one. I told them next week we would revisit and see how their solution is working. Then we talked about plans for the upcoming week and worked on what we are doing for Labor Day. I got some meal suggestions from them for my menu next week. By the time we were done my two kids were sitting there chatting away with each other about their day and it was such an awesome feeling to sit back and look at that. No animosity, no name-calling, nothing hurtful. By the time the alarm rang for the end of the meeting, we were all in such a great mood. We planned that our meetings would work better on Wednesday evenings and I think they are actually looking forward to them. One small step. . . . :-)*

We live in a very "speeded up" society. It is easy to get sidetracked from what is most important to you—your family. Making the effort and taking the time to hold regular family meetings can help maintain a balance of priorities and all the other little things that need to be done.

## A WORD OF ENCOURAGEMENT: DON'T EXPECT PERFECTION

One final tip regarding family meetings: don't expect perfection. It takes time for family members to believe that their thoughts and ideas are important to others. It takes time for them to learn the skills for successful family meetings. However, nothing is more powerful to create family respect, cooperation, and lasting memories than family meetings. It can be more fun to read old family meeting journals (lists of compliments, problems, and solutions) than it is to look at family photo albums.

### KIND AND FIRM PARENTING TOOLS TO REMEMBER

1. Instead of dealing with issues in the heat of the moment, use family meetings to work out issues after cooling off. Putting an item on the agenda allows for cooling-off time before the family meeting occurs.
2. Family meetings are worth the effort because of the high degree of belonging and significance your teens will feel as a result of participating.
3. Family meetings are good places for discussion without worrying about coming up with a solution.
4. Family meetings work best when held regularly and not in the middle of a crisis or at the whim of a parent.
5. Unless you can reach a consensus about an issue, don't initiate any new family procedures. Stick with what you currently are doing or, as a parent, decide how it will be temporarily. Then, keep the discussion open until all family members come up with something they can all live with.
6. Use family meetings to discuss any and all topics, whether mundane or extraordinary.

### Practical Application Activity

At first, family members may feel uncomfortable with complimenting, or think it is silly. If you have faith in the process and give your family members opportunities to practice at the start of each week's family meeting, skills will grow, and so will the good feelings in your family. To get your family started, use this activity at a family meeting.

1. Ask family members to think of a time when someone said something that made them feel good about themselves. Take turns sharing the examples.

2. Ask family members to think of something for which they would like to receive a compliment. Remind everyone that sometimes it helps to ask for what you want so that you get noticed for what is really important to you.

3. Ask family members to say what they would like to be complimented on and then invite the others to give the compliment. For example, your teen might want a compliment on how he or she remembered to return the car with gas in the tank (even though it might be only a dollar's worth). Dad says, "Thank you for being thoughtful about returning the car with gas in the tank. It's nice to be able to get to work in the morning without having to stop at the gas station." Notice that Dad doesn't say anything about how little fuel there is in the tank.

4. Remind family members that when receiving a compliment, it is helpful to say, "Thanks," so the person giving the compliment knows it was received.

5. At another family meeting, you could suggest that family members take turns giving appreciations by starting with, "Thank you for . . ." or "I appreciate . . ." or "You make my life richer or easier because . . ."

# 8

# HOW CAN YOU SPEND SPECIAL TIME WITH YOUR TEEN?

## THE MAGIC OF TIME THAT COUNTS

During the teen years, when your children spend less and less time with you, it's more important than ever to connect in ways that really count. We call it "special time." Special time is different from the regular time you spend with your teen in that it is a scheduled time that is as sacred as any important meeting. Unfortunately, several conditions make special time difficult to achieve: busy schedules, teenagers' preference to be with their friends, and time spent lecturing, judging, and punishing.

Brian decided to try spending special time with his son, Ted. Brian's attempts to control Ted's use of drugs and alcohol had damaged their relationship. He had grounded Ted, taken away his car, and lectured ad infinitum ("How could you do such a thing? You'll ruin your life forever.

What have we done wrong?"), but all to no avail. Ted got more defiant and more rebellious, and the father-son relationship deteriorated badly.

Brian was thoroughly discouraged, but decided to take a class called "Positive Discipline for Teens" before giving up completely. The very first night of the class he heard something that would later change his life, as well as his son's. The facilitator said, "Sometimes you get the best results by forgetting about behavior and focusing on the relationship." The group leader went on to talk about connection before correction, explaining that creating closeness and trust instead of distance and hostility by making sure the message of love gets through is extremely important with teens. Brian thought that sounded pretty simplistic, but he also realized that trying to improve his relationship with his son certainly couldn't do any harm.

The next day, Brian showed up at Ted's school during his lunch period and got permission to take his son to lunch. Brian had decided that his whole purpose would be to enjoy Ted's company—no matter what. When Ted saw his dad, he asked belligerently, "What are you doing here?" Brian replied, "I just wanted to have lunch with you."

During lunch, Brian focused on his purpose, avoiding third-degree questions. He didn't even ask Ted how his day was. Ted was suspicious all during lunch, waiting to be criticized or lectured. The entire lunch was spent in silence. Afterward, Brian took Ted back to school and said, "Thanks for having lunch with me. I really enjoyed being with you." Ted walked into school with a bewildered look on his face.

Brian continued showing up at Ted's school for lunch every Wednesday. It took three weeks for Ted's suspicions to disappear. He then started telling his father small things about his day, and his father did the same. Ted even began asking questions about work and college. Brian was careful to answer Ted's questions without lecturing.

Meanwhile, Brian had stopped trying to control Ted through punishment and withdrawal of privileges at home. Instead, he focused on Ted's assets, even though he had to dig to get past his fears about Ted's rebellion. He told Ted how glad he was to have him as his son and described to Ted how thrilled he had been the day he was born. Brian found it easy to tell stories about the cute things Ted had done as a child. Ted would shrug and give the impression that he thought these stories were "stupid." However, during this time, Brian noticed that Ted showed up for dinner more often and sometimes brought his friends over to watch television.

One day, three months into the lunch routine, Brian got stuck in a meeting that lasted through the lunch period. That night, Ted said, "What happened to you today, Dad?"

Brian apologized, "I'm sorry. I didn't know you were expecting me. We never said it would be a regular thing. But I'd love to make it a regular routine; how about you?"

Nonchalantly, Ted said, "Sure."

Brian said, "I'll be sure to leave a message if I ever get tied up again."

Brian felt pleased and gratified about the effectiveness of spending special time with his son. He didn't know if Ted stopped experimenting with drugs and alcohol, but he knew his control efforts hadn't worked. Now, at least, the damaged relationship was being repaired, and Brian was grateful that the importance of this had gotten through his own thick skull. He felt satisfied that he was providing good memories for his son and letting him know from experience that his father loved him unconditionally. Ted's behavior improved considerably. He stopped being disrespectful. In fact, he started being considerate about letting his parents know when he would be home. Brian was creating an atmosphere in which his son could think more about how his behavior affected his life rather than spending so much energy on "getting even" with his dad for the lectures and criticism.

## FIND A WAY TO SPEND SPECIAL TIME THAT WORKS FOR YOU AND YOUR TEEN

Participants at an "Empowering Teens and Yourself in the Process" workshop brainstormed the following list of ideas for spending special time with teenagers. They based this list on an understanding of teens.

## IDEAS FOR SPENDING SPECIAL TIME TOGETHER

Listen without judging

Validate their feelings

Stop nagging

Take extended trips

Go on day trips

Take walks together

Do activities planned by them

Tell stories about your own childhood

Watch their television programs

Look at photo albums of when they were little

Listen to their music together

Work on mutual respect

Invite them to see you at your job

Do activities of their choice with them

Support their activities and interests

Share about yourself if they're interested

Include them in your discussions

Work on joint problem solving

Schedule regular family meetings

Ski or snowboard together

Practice role reversal and role-playing

Allow them to make their own mistakes

Show interest in their world

Backpack together

Hang out with them

Work less, play more, be available

Go to concerts or ball games

Go to a flea market

Work on creative projects (arts and crafts)

Ask for their opinions

Cook together

Make home a comfortable place for their friends

Keep a sense of humor

Remember that differences are okay

Take care of yourself and your own issues

Go to a retreat together

Shop with them

Treat them to activities they enjoy but can't afford

Take time off from work to be with your teens

Eat together or go out to a restaurant

Play games together

Ask for their help

Spend special time alone with each child

Plan an event together

Plan vacations ("What do you want to do?")

Have faith

Have trust

Laugh a lot

We suggest referring to this list often. It may inspire you to spend special time with your teenagers in ways you haven't thought of or that get lost in the shuffle of busy lives. End every family meeting by planning at least one family activity from this list or from a list that comes out of your own family's brainstorming (see Chapter 7).

Short periods (even minutes) of quality time a day, a week, or even a month can do wonders to improve your relationships with your teens. Focusing on spending quality time with your teens will help you remember to get into their world, see them with perspective, and bring back the joy of being a parent.

During therapy, we often recommend that parents spend quality time with their kids, but it doesn't always happen. And when it doesn't, surprisingly, the young people often tattle that their parents haven't done their homework. One excited preteen announced in a session, "Mom finally did that thing you were saying—that 'special time.' It was so much fun."

"What did you do?" her therapist asked, thinking that they went out to dinner or to the movies as they had discussed week after week.

"We lit about a hundred candles, put the stereo on really loud, and danced around in the living room. We're going to do it again sometime, aren't we, Mom? It was the best!"

What parent wouldn't want to create some quality time with their teen when they get results like that!

## HANG OUT AND JUST BE AVAILABLE

Remember Brian who took time each week to take his son out to lunch? He demonstrated true dedication by being willing to take time off from work to make his son a priority.

We've found it can be equally effective just to "hang out," to be available at certain times when you know your kids will be around. The pitfall is expecting that your teens will notice, or care, or that they will talk to you. Even if it seems they don't notice, the energy you create when you're truly available is different from that when you're "there" but preoccupied with other concerns or too busy to be bothered.

Teenagers can tell when you expect something from them—and expectations can create resistance. We've heard many parents complain, "Well, I'm available, but my teenager still won't talk to me." Hanging out means being available to listen if your teens want to talk—and if they don't. It means being a "closet" listener (not making it obvious that you're listening). It means listening to who they are rather than focusing on their words. Five helpful tips will increase your chances of making the time you spend hanging out with your teenager count as quality time.

## TIPS FOR SPENDING TIME THAT COUNTS

For at least five minutes a day, spend time with your teenager while keeping

1. your mouth shut (listening).
2. your sense of humor intact (perspective).
3. your ears open (curiosity).
4. your heart emanating warmth and gratitude (love).
5. a desire to understand your teen's world (focusing).

Imagine the effect on your teenager of receiving five minutes a day or less of special time.

Grandpa Louie was visiting his daughter and her stepson, Rico. Grandpa was very encouraging because he could see past the surface behavior to the good in others. Rico stayed out late, left his room in chaos, ran out of gas, got bad grades, and was usually in trouble for one thing or another. Every time Grandpa saw Rico, he said, "Rico, you're all right!" Rico looked at him quizzically, waiting for the catch, even as the corners of his mouth turned up. Grandpa Louie must have told Rico he was "all right" at least a hundred times, until Rico looked at him and said, "Grandpa, I know what you're going to say . . . I'm all right. Right?" Grandpa just looked

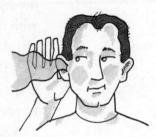

up and grinned. This special time that Grandpa spent with Rico was un-scheduled and took only seconds at a time. However, the boost to Rico's self-confidence was immeasurable in an environment where he was hearing so many negative comments.

Hugs are another way to take only seconds for time that counts. With teens, be sure you don't hug them in front of anyone else. You may even have to use your sense of humor and say, "I know you can't stand hugs from me right now, but I might die without one. Could you please spare your dignity for three seconds to save my life?"

## SPECIAL TIME AND SIBLING RIVALRY

Children feel special when you care enough to spend one-on-one time with them. Although you know it is important to spend time with each of them individually as well as during family time, it's not always easy to do. A child may feel threatened by your desire to spend one-on-one time with another child and create a scene or diversion so you will include him or give him time instead of his sibling.

Arnel and Jack were parents to fifteen-year-old Kelsey and ten-year-old Cassie. Kelsey was at the height of her teen behavior, spending endless hours in her room away from the family. Cassie demanded lots of attention and usually got it, even if it was negative attention. Whenever Arnel or Jack tried to spend time with Kelsey, Cassie pitched a fit and Kelsey headed for her room and slammed the door. The parents weren't happy with this situation and decided to do something about it.

Talking about the issue at the family meeting fell on deaf ears. One day, the parents read in the local paper that there was going to be a big grape-stomping contest at a nearby fair. They asked the girls if they'd like to participate, and to their surprise, both girls gave a hearty yes.

When the day of the contest arrived, the family dressed in matching T-shirts. Arnel volunteered to be the photographer, and Jack volunteered to take a turn with each girl during different rounds of the competition. The girls drew straws to see who would be first. As their round was called, they climbed into the barrel filled with grapes and started stomping, splattering Jack and themselves with grape juice. Jack was on the outside of the barrel reaching his arm in to keep the drain open so the juice could flow freely. Arnel was just out of harm's way snapping photos. At the end of the competition, laughing and teasing, Jack and the girls hosed each other down to get rid of as much grape juice as they could.

Arnel posted the pictures on her Facebook account, and later, after the family recovered from their big day, she said, "I know that sometimes you girls are jealous of each other and wondering if we spend more time with one or the other. In the future, if you feel jealous, I hope you'll look at the pictures of you guys covered in grape juice and remember how much fun it was to do something special with the family. Maybe we could think of something we could do every week that would be 'special time' for us. I'll take lots of pictures and we can post them where everyone can see."

This event was a huge breakthrough for this family. We encourage you to create a connection with your teens by spending time that counts so that you will know how to encourage your teen, and your teen will feel unconditionally loved.

## KIND AND FIRM PARENTING TOOLS TO REMEMBER

1. When it's the hardest to spend time with your teen, it's very important that the time you do spend is quality, lecture-free time.
2. Don't expect your teens to be open with you if you don't have a good relationship first. A good relationship takes time for getting to know who your teens are instead of telling them how you want them to be.
3. Just hanging out, which means being around, available, and without an agenda, seems the best way to start spending time with your teen.
4. Keep the "Ideas for Spending Special Time Together" list (page 125) handy so you and your teen can find ways to enjoy being together on a regular basis.

*Practical Application Activity*

If you did nothing more than remember to have fun with your teenagers on a regular basis, you would be surprised how much your relationships would improve—and how much more you would enjoy life in general. Unfortunately, you can get caught up in busy schedules and in dealing with problems. This activity serves as a reminder of the importance of having fun and provides inspiration and motivation to do it.

Look back at the list called "Ideas for Spending Special Time Together." Check off some of the activities that appeal to you. Now give the list to your teens and ask them to check off, in a different color, activities that appeal to them. Then ask others in the family to do the same.

Schedule a "Fun Things to Do" meeting, and bring the list. Circle the items that more than one person has marked.

Brainstorm more fun things that all family members have in common. Add those items to the list.

Each member of the family then presents one thing that he or she would like to do for fun as a family. If the rest of the family agrees to participate, schedule the event on a calendar on a date that suits everyone. There should be a date planned for each member of the family's favorite activity. Then have fun together.

# 9

# ARE YOU ENABLING OR EMPOWERING YOUR TEEN?

## PREPARING TEENS FOR LIFE

Let's face it. Sometimes it feels great to have others spoil us, do things for us we could do for ourselves, and take care of us. However, when parents do these things with their teens, it is called "enabling"—behaviors that stop teens from being capable. As much as teens complain about their parents being too controlling, they might not be too excited if their parents have been "enabling" and suddenly become "empowering."

What's the difference? Enabling is doing for kids what they can do for themselves. It's intervening between your kid and life experience. Enabling behaviors usually come from fear or worry or guilt or shame. They subtly demonstrate a lack of trust in teens to be able to handle life experiences.

Empowering, on the other hand, is stepping out of the middle between life and your kids but being available on the sidelines for support and encouragement. It is giving kids a hand when they "fall down" because they made a mistake, or need a boost when they are working hard to help themselves. It's also doing *with* them instead of *for* them. You learn to be a good copilot, showing faith and trust in them to be able to do what they need to, but being available if asked. Empowering behaviors give kids practice to learn from mistakes and build their "capability" muscles.

If you always rescue or try to control your teens, what will happen when you aren't around? How are you preparing them for life? If you never allow your teens to fail, how will they learn how to recover from failure? If you don't allow your teens to experience the consequences of their choices in a supportive atmosphere (through validating feelings and curiosity questions), how will they experience the consequences of their choices when you aren't around?

This chapter teaches the tools for empowering teens. It provides a foundation on which teens can build their inner resources. (Punishments and rewards teach dependence on outer sources.) Your highest achievement as a parent is to make your job obsolete—to not be needed, to help your teen learn the characteristics and life skills he or she needs to survive independently. By using long-term parenting, parents empower instead of enable their teens.

## TYPICAL ENABLING BEHAVIORS

Waking teens in the morning, doing their laundry, fixing their lunches, picking out their clothes.

Loaning money and/or giving extra money after teens have spent their allowance or used specially earmarked funds, such as a clothing allowance, on something else.

Typing papers, researching, delivering forgotten homework or lunches to school.

Lying to teachers when teens cut classes or skip school.

Feeling sorry for teens when they have a lot of homework
or activities, excusing them from helping the family with
household chores.

Pretending everything is fine, when it clearly isn't, to avoid
confrontation.

Giving them everything they want—"because everyone else
has one."

## TYPICAL EMPOWERING BEHAVIORS

Listening and giving emotional support and validation
without fixing or discounting.

Teaching life skills.

Working on agreements through family meetings or the joint
problem-solving process.

Letting go (without abandoning).

Deciding what you will do, with dignity and respect.

Sharing what you think, how you feel, and what you want
without lecturing, moralizing, insisting on agreement, or
demanding satisfaction.

Sometimes parents think the preceding empowering suggestions feel
like "doing nothing" because they don't include punishment or control.
However, when parents follow these suggestions, they are doing a great
deal to ensure long-term results. As you look at the two previous lists,
you may become vividly aware of how skilled you are in enabling responses and how unskilled you are in empowering responses. Enabling
responses seem to be second nature to most parents.

During our experiential workshops and classes we ask for nineteen
volunteers—nine volunteers will form a line of "enabling parents," and
nine volunteers will form a line of "empowering parents." One volunteer
will play the role of a teen.

We then ask the "teen" to walk down the line of "enabling parents"
who make the following statements regarding homework, while the

"teen" just notices what he or she is thinking, feeling, and deciding in response to the statements.

## ENABLING STATEMENTS

1. "I can't believe you have procrastinated again. What will ever become of you? Okay, I'll do it this time, but next time you'll just have to suffer the consequences."

2. "Honey, I thought you would do your homework after I bought you a car, a cell phone, and a big allowance."

3. "You can have a new CD, allowance, cell phone, if you do your homework."

4. "Honey, you hurry and do as much as you can now while I pick out your clothes, and warm up the car so you won't be cold when I drive you to school."

5. "I just don't understand. I excused you from chores, I woke you up early, I drove you everywhere so you would have more time; I made your lunches. How could this be?"

6. "Okay, I'll write a note to the teacher that you were sick this morning, but you'll need to be sure and catch up."

7. "Well then, you are grounded and you lose all your privileges, no car, no TV, no friends, until it is done."

8. "Well, no wonder. I saw you wasting your time on the boob tube and spending too much time with your friends and sleeping in. You should feel ashamed of yourself. You'd better shape up or you'll be shipping out to live on the streets like a bum."

9. "How many times have I told you to get your homework done early? Why can't you be more like your brother? Why can't you be more responsible? What will become of you?"

Imagine you are a teen who has just heard these statements. What would you be thinking, feeling, and deciding? Would you feel empowered? Would you be thinking about how helpful and encouraging these statements are? Would you be deciding that you could hardly wait to do better? We think not. People who participate in this activity as a teen say they felt shut down, rebellious, angry, turned off, and tuned out.

Now stay as a teen in your imagination and notice what you are thinking, feeling, and deciding as you listen to the "empowering statements."

## EMPOWERING STATEMENTS

1. "What is your picture of what is going on regarding your homework? Would you be willing to hear my concerns? Could we brainstorm together on some possible solutions?"

2. "I can see that you feel bad about getting that poor grade. I have faith in you to learn from this and figure out what you need to do to get the grade you want."

3. "I'm not willing to bail you out. When your teacher calls, I'll hand the phone to you so she can discuss it with you." (A respectful attitude and tone of voice is essential.)

4. "I would like to hear what this means for you."

5. "I'm willing to be available for an hour two nights a week when we agree in advance on a convenient time, but I'm not willing to get involved at the last minute."

6. "I hope you'll go to college, but I'm not sure it's important to you. I'm happy to talk with you about your thoughts or plans about college."

7. "I'm feeling too upset to talk about this right now. Let's put it on the agenda for the family meeting so we can talk about it when I'm not so emotional."

8. "Could we sit down and see if we can work on a plan regarding homework that we both can live with?"

9. "I love you just the way you are and respect you to choose what is right for you."

Our guess is that you are now feeling more empowered in the role as a teen, that you are thinking your parent really loves you and has faith in

you to be capable and to learn from your mistakes, and that it is okay to think for yourself and that you want to do what is best to improve your life. Participants in this activity tell us when they played the teen they felt surprised and had stopped to think about how to take responsibility rather than being reactive.

## EMPOWERMENT: THE FOUNDATION OF LONG-TERM PARENTING

We often ask parents to tell us what life skills they want for their kids. They reply with words like "self-discipline," "responsibility," "account-ability," "self-confidence and courage," "desire to cooperate and contribute," "communication and problem-solving skills," "self-motivation to learn," "honesty," "sense of humor," "happy," "healthy self-esteem," "flexible," "resilient," "curious," "respect for self and others," "empathy," "compassion," and "belief in personal capability." After going through the list of enabling and empowering questions, ask your teen what he or she is learning about these qualities from the enabling parent and then from the empowering parent. No surprises here. From the enabling parents, the teens aren't learning much and sort of merrily go on their way with no sense of personal responsibility. From the empowering parents, the teens are experiencing many of the qualities and behaviors on the life skills list above.

The courage that is developed from empowerment is resiliency, the ability to cope when the going gets tough. Teens experience extremes in emotion, changes of loyalty from parents to friends, and a whole new world of temptations. Some teens go to the extreme of suicide because they lack the courage to deal with tough problems. These teens haven't learned that mistakes and failures are not the end of the world, but are opportunities to learn.

## TO HELP ESTABLISH COURAGE IN TEENS

- Have faith in them and in yourself.

- Let them know that mistakes are opportunities to learn.

- Give them opportunities to try again, rather than punishing or rescuing them.

- Work on agreements, solutions, and plans to overcome problems.

- Show them that what happens now is only for now and that tomorrow is another day to apply what they learned today.

Most people think a responsible teen is a perfect teen. This is not true. Responsibility is the ability to face mistakes and to use them as opportunities for growth. Responsibility is the knowledge that you are accountable for your behavior and that your actions and choices affect your life.

## TO HELP ESTABLISH RESPONSIBILITY IN TEENS

- Be consciously irresponsible (don't do things for them and don't nag them).

- Help them explore the consequences of their choices through friendly discussions and curiosity questions.

- Don't punish them for mistakes.

- Teach problem-solving skills for correcting mistakes.

- Don't pamper them to help them avoid pain. (In the process of dealing with their pain, they develop courage and experience the feeling of capability.)

- Teach accountability with kindness and firmness at the same time.

- Maintain your sense of humor and help your teens stop taking themselves and others so seriously.

Positive Discipline associate Kelly Pfeiffer (www.thinkitthroughparenting .com) came up with twenty ways to help your teenager be and feel capable. Here are some of her suggestions:

1. Ask your teen to cook one night a week.
2. Stop doing laundry for teens. Teach them how to do their own.
3. Allow your teen to go to a dentist or other appointments alone.
4. Let your teen pump the gas and check the oil.
5. Show teens how to make their own appointments and stand nearby while they do it.
6. Never hesitate to say, "This is something you can do on your own." Or, "I believe you can do this. I'll be happy to show you how to get started."

The following options will help you understand the difference between enabling and empowering regarding specific parent/teen issues. You may prefer small steps for empowering, or you may be ready to take a bigger leap. (There is more than one choice under each heading.) Once you understand the spirit of what we are saying, you can use your own creativity. Your success will depend on the degree to which you stay in the present, focus on what you can do today, and give up worrying about how your teen will turn out. The life skills you teach today build character for tomorrow.

## CARS AND DRIVING

### Enabling

Buy your teen a car. Pay for all gas and insurance. Then try to control him or her by threats about taking away the car if grades don't improve.

### Small Steps for Empowering

Make agreements about how to share the family car. Let the kids know that you'll expect them to run errands for you or drive siblings places if you share your car with them.

Let your teen drive you around so you can research (with your mouth shut) your teen's skills and confidence. If you do have tips, ask if your teen would like to hear them.

Involve your teen in caring for the family car.

Share your teen's interest and excitement by looking through car magazines together or shopping car lots.

Make a list of all expenses involved in having a car. Be clear about what expenses you will cover (and then stick to it even if your teen gets into trouble).

### Bigger Steps for Empowering

Expect teens to save for at least half the cost of a car and pay for part of their insurance or get a good student discount to lower the insurance rate.

Give your teen an old car to use and care for as soon as he or she can earn enough money to pay for gas and has good enough grades to lower insurance.

Take time for training how your teen can manage without a car by learning how to use public transportation.

Let your teens ride in cars with their friends so they don't need a car of their own.

Research insurance rates together and the difference in rates with a "good student" discount.

Expect your teen to help cover the deductible for any accidents and to be involved in setting up the repair process.

Let your teen take you on a road trip.

Work together on agreements about where, when, and how a car can be used—even if your teen used his or her own money.

## SIBLINGS AND FIGHTING

### Enabling

Get involved in all fights. Take sides as if you know for sure who started it. Punish the "guilty one" and favor the "innocent." This is excellent "bully/victim" training.

### Small Steps for Empowering

Talk with your teen about how he or she feels about siblings.

Notice if you let one of your children get away with more than the other.

Look at your own sibling issues and figure out how they might color your parenting

Don't expect older siblings to parent younger siblings.

Don't punish a sibling for the mistakes another sibling makes.

### Bigger Steps for Empowering

Schedule regular family meetings where your teen learns to give and receive compliments.

Stay out of siblings' fights. Or if the fighting is physical and the kids can't work it out, create a system where both kids need to be in separate rooms until they are ready to stop fighting.

Suggest that siblings put problems on the family meeting agenda so the whole family can help brainstorm possible solutions.

Avoid good kid/bad kid labels and let the teens know that you expect both of them to work out the issue and that you're willing to help or hire a therapist to help.

Let siblings create a plan together about who rides in the front seat or sits by the window, how to divide shared rooms, and scheduling for their favorite TV programs if they differ.

Appreciate and encourage differences. Never compare one child with another.

## PARTIES

### Enabling

Forbid your teens to attend parties. Believe them when they tell you they are "staying with a friend."

### Small Steps for Empowering

Talk about your fears. Ask your teen to explain to you why kids like parties.

Remember your teen years.

Plan parties with teens and their parents in your home.

Plan some parties with your teen at which you will make yourself scarce (in the house, but with your door shut). Do not turn the house over to the kids without an adult present.

Read articles about what teens say about parties.

Never leave your house without an adult over a weekend.

Volunteer for "project graduation" nights.

Take your teen to "First Nights" for New Year's Eve.

Make a deal that if your teen drinks, you'll pick him or her up, no questions asked.

### Bigger Steps for Empowering

Ask your teen how he or she plans to behave at parties. Role-play what your teen will do if he or she feels uncomfortable. Set up a code phrase your teen can use to call for help, for example, "I forgot to feed the dog."

Get real. Teens party. For many, their idea of a party is a place without parents and possibly with beer, wine, alcohol, and other drugs. There may be some sexual activity. You don't have to like it, and you can try to stop it, but maybe it would be better to hold some honest discussions with your teen to keep the lines of communication open. That way, if your teen needs you, you will be someone to talk to without fear of judgment.

Know your teen. Have faith in your teen. Teach your teen skills so he or she will know how to deal with situations and to have the self-confidence to do what is right for him- or herself.

Ask to know who the designated driver is and who is going to stay sober to make sure nothing dangerous or disrespectful happens if someone passes out.

## CLOTHING, HAIR, TATTOOS, PIERCINGS, GAUGING

### Enabling

Engage in power struggles about what your teens can and can't do. Use threats, punishments, and rewards in an attempt to get them to live your ideas of how they should look.

### Small Steps for Empowering

Sit in your car outside your teen's school and observe the other students.

Go to the mall and observe what teens are wearing, including tattoos, piercings, and gauging.

Look at your own materialism. Set up a clothing allowance, and stick to it.

Allow your teen to learn from mistakes if he or she goes over budget. Don't lecture or judge.

Remind yourself that your teen won't carry the "teen look" into adulthood (except for tattoos and gauging, which can be repaired through surgery).

Set up an appointment for your teen with a hairdresser or makeup specialist.

Go to the Internet with your teen and research the safest place to get piercings, and so on, done, the cost, the pain, the healing process, the removal process if your teen has a change of heart later.

Set an age you feel comfortable with or expect your teen to wait till they are eighteen.

Realize tattoos, piercings, gauging are parts of teen belonging and significance rituals and a sign to them they are growing up.

Use curiosity questions with your teen. "What is it about the 'look' that is important to you? How do you think you'll feel about the 'look' when you are an adult? (Is there any possibility that your preferences might change?)"

### Bigger Steps for Empowering

Enjoy the look; take pictures.

If your teen pays no attention to hygiene, set up a routine together and use follow-through.

Let your teen choose his or her own look, but ask for give-and-take when you want him or her to dress special for something important to you.

Plan a shopping trip together (out of town so your teen's friends won't see you both at the mall together—God forbid!). Let your teen choose where to shop.

Throw away your TV so your teen isn't so influenced by all the advertising.

Go with your teen to discuss tattoos, piercings, gauging with the artist who might be the person doing the job—including the cost of removal if your teen changes his or her mind later.

Be honest about what you want or don't want, while letting your teen know that you prefer they don't do anything that changes their body until you both agree. Keep the dialogue open until you find that win/win.

If your teen sneaks and comes home with a tattoo against your wishes, get out the camera and say, "I love you no matter what." Share something you did as a teen that your parents did not like.

## CURFEW

### Enabling

Set curfews without any input from your teen. Ground your teen whenever he or she does not keep the curfew—but don't follow through with the grounding.

Give up and let your teen do what he or she wants.

### Small Steps for Empowering

Set a curfew and let your teen know that it is open for discussion, as long as you both agree.

Let your teen know you will be flexible as long as he or she respects your need to feel secure.

Call other parents to find out what time they set curfew (instead of simply accepting, "All the other parents let their kids . . .").

Get a group of parents and teens together in your home for an open discussion about curfew and about what will work for everyone.

### Bigger Steps for Empowering

Let your teen tell you what time he or she will be home each night. Stick with that as long as it is working. If it stops working, set a curfew and let your teen know you will return to the old system and try again when you both feel ready.

Talk about curfew as a respect issue, the way you would with a roommate. Ask your teen to call if he or she will be late.

Don't be afraid to say no if your teen needs a night home to regroup. Sometimes you have to be the "bad guy," when your teen has been burning the candle at both ends and is exhausted but just can't stop. This might happen once or twice a year.

Know your teen. This happens when you engage in regular curiosity questions, family meetings, role-playing what to do in difficult situations, special time, and joint problem solving.

Express your faith in your teen to think about what he or she is doing and how it will affect his or her life.

# MONEY

### Enabling

Give your teen an ample allowance without any discussion about how he or she will spend it. When your teen runs out, give the "I can't afford it" lecture and then give him or her more money with the promise that you won't do this again.

### Small Steps for Empowering

Start your teen on an allowance that is not connected to chores.

Avoid bailouts. Allow your teen to learn from spending mistakes.

Pay for work you would hire someone else to do. Pay only after the work is done and done to your standards.

If you make loans, start with small amounts and keep a payment ledger to track repayment. Do not loan larger amounts until your teen establishes his or her creditworthiness with you.

Expect your teen to come up with a matching amount before you put in your share of a purchase. ("You save half and I'll save half.")

### Bigger Steps for Empowering

Discuss together what your teen is expected to cover with his or her allowance. Do not provide increases until your teen makes a proposal that makes sense to you.

Provide a clothing allowance twice a year. If your teen runs out of money and wants more, show empathy and then faith that he or she can figure out how to make the next clothing allowance work better.

Expect your teens to find part-time work (a few hours a week) to help pay for their expenses.

Expect your teens to help pay for cell-phone use. Even a small amount helps build responsibility.

## CHORES

### Enabling
Don't expect your kids to do any chores. It just isn't worth the power struggles, and they're only young once.

### Small Steps for Empowering
Expect all your children to do chores.

During a family meeting, get your teen involved in brainstorming who, how, and when the chores should be done.

Create routine chore charts together.

Use follow-through to make sure the chores get done.

Avoid excuses, even if there is a test the next day. Expect your teen to schedule time to help with chores. You can always offer to trade or help out on special occasions.

### Bigger Steps for Empowering
Get your teen involved in cooking, grocery shopping, doing laundry, making lunch, ironing, caring for the car, cleaning house, and anything else that will prepare your teen for being an adult.

Respect your teen's busy schedule, but insist that he or she finds at least one night to cook no matter how simple the menu.

## ROOMS

### Enabling
Nag and lecture about your teen's messy room. Threaten and bribe, but don't follow through.

### Small Steps for Empowering

Go to a storage store with your teen to pick out hooks and other storage items.

Let your teen decorate part of the rooms in the house.

Expect your teen's room to be cleaned once a week. Offer a choice for your teen to clean alone or with your help.

### Bigger Steps for Empowering

Let your teens keep the bedrooms the way they want. Expect teens to bring all dishes, glasses, and so on to the kitchen at least once a week and set a deadline for when that will be. Follow through on the deadline.

Trust your teen will clean the bedroom when ready. (Some of the messiest teens become the tidiest adults—and some stay messy.)

Come up with a budget for painting, posters, and bedding. Let your teen redecorate the room.

## DATING AND SEX

### Enabling

Stick your head in the sand and pretend your teen will not get involved in sex.

### Small Steps for Empowering

Don't overreact; they'll probably break up within a week—if you stay out of it.

Understand that "going steady" means different things for different ages. Find out what it means for your teen.

Do the same about sex. Your teen may have a very different definition of "sex" than you do.

Talk to your teens about birth control, telling them your thoughts and finding out theirs. Your teen may be ready to have sex, but not babies. Even if your kids aren't ready for sex, it's going on around them and they need a place to talk about their concerns.

With preteens, drive them to the movies or the mall and pick them up.

Let your teen have pool parties or other coed gatherings with you as a chaperone.

Promote group activities.

Include your teen's date in family activities.

### Bigger Steps for Empowering

If your teen feels ready to date, let it be, but stay involved and vigilant and be open to discussions.

Make sure you discuss your fears and thoughts about teenage sex and unprotected sex, and listen carefully to your teen's thoughts.

Have a discussion about how some girls think they have to have sex with a boyfriend to avoid rejection. Encourage them to know what they want and have the wisdom to know that they might want to consider rejecting anyone who might reject them for not having sex.

Engage teens in role-playing possible scenarios they might find themselves in—such as feeling passionate in the backseat of a car. Help them think through what they want for now *and* the future.

If your teen wants to be sexually active, offer to go with him or her to get birth control. Teens may not be embarrassed to have sex, but they hesitate to talk to you about it, fearing judgment.

Educate your teens about date rape and encourage them to always have a sober friend who serves as watchdog.

Make sure your teen feels loved. Otherwise your teen might feel the need to look for "love" in the wrong places.

## SCHOOL

### Enabling

Demonstrate by your words and actions that your teen's grades are more important to you than he or she is. Micromanage homework. Tell your teen when and where to do homework. Take away privileges if he or she doesn't get good grades. Go online and check how your teen is doing in school at least once a day.

### Small Steps for Empowering

Have a special time of day when the entire family does quiet work.

Create routines with your teen instead of micromanaging.

Read as a family.

Take classes together.

Take classes yourself.

Remember that the purpose of school is to learn, not necessarily to get the best grades and turn in the most papers.

Let your teen know that he or she is more important to you than school grades.

If grades go down, be a friend and look for the underlying reasons.

Be realistic about your teen's capabilities and don't expect your teens to have the same goals as you. Parents may think straight A's are imperative, but teens may think it's a waste of energy to work that hard in classes they aren't interested in and may be satisfied with a C.

Do not withdraw the things your teen is good at as punishment or what you think is "motivation."

Stay out of their homework as much as possible and hire tutors if they need help unless you are the rare parent who can help without fighting.

### Bigger Steps for Empowering

School isn't for everyone, and some teens may work better with home schooling or an online school or by taking an equivalency test and returning to school later.

Offer to help with schoolwork at certain times that fit your schedule, but let school be between your teen and the teachers as much as possible. Let your teen take the lead and notify you if a project involves parental help. Schedule times you can both work on the project.

Ask for school conferences that include both you and your teen to find out what is going on. Listen to all points of view. Focus on your teen and the teacher coming up with solutions rather than jumping in and taking over.

Don't overreact when your son or daughter gets detention or a bad grade; wait and see what your teen does about it and be available and encouraging without taking over.

Offer tutors when needed or when you and your teen fight while doing homework.

Appreciate each child's efforts as a learner, regardless of how accomplished or far along he or she is.

Encourage your teen to build on strengths. Don't harp on your teen to be good at everything.

## ELECTRONICS (CELL PHONES, COMPUTERS, VIDEO GAMES, TVS, IPODS, IPADS, AND WHATEVER ELSE IS INVENTED IN THE NEXT FEW MONTHS)

### Enabling

Be sure your teen has every new electronic gadget that comes along. Allow him or her to have all these gadgets in his or her room without any supervision.

### Small Steps for Empowering

Limit media time spent on computers, television, and computer games. At a family meeting, thoughtfully schedule time for these activities with your teens.

Use the parental controls on Internet servers.

Talk with teens about the danger and the value of chatting with people they don't know. Ask for ideas on how your teen can protect him- or herself from the potential dangers of online chats.

Do not buy a television for your teen's bedroom.

Remember that teens today see more explicit sex and violence on TV and in the movies than ever before. You may not be able to protect your teen from this, but you can engage in friendly discussions about what your teen is watching and about what your teen thinks about it.

Ask your teen to teach you computer skills.

Do not eat meals while watching TV. Save this special mealtime for friendly conversation.

Have a nighttime "parking lot" for all electronics (especially games and cell phones). This electronics parking lot could also be used during specified time of the day (homework time and mealtimes).

**Bigger Steps for Empowering**

Eliminate all TVs, except for use with thoughtfully rented DVDs or streaming devices. (We know—this is a very big step but we meet families who are TV free and love it.)

If you aren't ready for the biggest step, at least occasionally if not constantly watch your teen's favorite programs with him or her, so you can be aware of what your teen is viewing. Ask how much your teen thinks the media influences what he or she thinks or does. Friendly discussions can help teens think about what they are seeing and verbalize it so they can come to some understanding of media's influence on them.

You do not have to buy a cell phone for your teens (unless you want them to have one for emergency use only). Work with teens to figure out how they can share the cost and how they will use a cell phone. If they want to load it with apps, have them set up their own iTunes account and invite relatives to give gift certificates for special occasions.

When your teen wants to buy products advertised on TV, help him or her think it through. "Why do you really want it? Can you pay for it? Are you being duped by consumerism?"

## THE MALL, CONCERTS, AND OTHER ACTIVITIES

### Enabling

Forbid your teen from going to any of the above, or let them go wherever they want without any supervision or discussions.

### Small Steps for Empowering

Understand that, in terms of socialization, the mall and concerts are as important to your teen as barn dances were for your grandparents.

Take your preteen to the mall; sit down by yourself with a soft drink or cup of coffee, and wait till he or she is ready to leave or meet at an agreed-upon time.

Occasionally go to concerts with your teens and their friends. Agree to sit in the back row so they don't have to be seen with you if that makes them more comfortable.

Take your teen to an audiologist (or research literature about audiology) for information about the danger to eardrums when exposed to excessively loud music. Ask for your teen's ideas on how to protect hearing.

### Bigger Steps for Empowering

Know your teens and have faith in them to use the skills you have helped them develop. They may rebel and make mistakes, but have faith in them to use the skills to decide what is right for them.

Once you have provided opportunities for your teen to learn skills and to know that you love him or her unconditionally, be thankful that you don't know everything your teen does—just as your parents didn't know everything you did.

Have faith in your teens to become fabulous adults (just as you did), even if you don't agree with their choice of music or current value system.

## FRIENDS, PEERS

### Enabling

Criticize your teen's friends. Tell your teen the kind of friends she should have. If your teen is an introvert and seems happy with just one friend, try to convince him why he should "get out" and make more friends. Push your teen into sports or activities you think would be "good for her."

### Small Steps for Empowering

Look at why teens might be choosing the friends they have. Do they feel insecure? Are they looking for friends who don't expect too much of them?

Provide many opportunities for your teen to develop perceptions of confidence and capability. This will translate into an ability to choose like-minded friends.

Don't criticize your teen's friends. Instead, invite them into your home where you can be a good influence.

If some of your teen's friends seem very scary to you, it is okay to trust your gut and let your teen know that these friends are welcome in your home, but only when you are there.

Accept your teen's style. You may have a teen who prefers one close friend instead of being part of the popular crowd.

### Bigger Steps for Empowering

Let your teens hang out with their friends behind the closed door of their bedrooms. (It is very disrespectful to assume that because the door is closed they are having orgies or doing drugs.)

It is okay to knock on the door during the evening and ask if you can come in. Teens will most likely say yes, and parents will probably find them sprawled on the floor or the bed listening to music, playing computer games, and talking.

If teens have trouble making friends, ask if they would like some hints. Otherwise, have faith in them to work it out.

If your teens want to drive their friends' places (once it's legal to do so), trust them to make that decision. If you think the friends are taking advantage of them, a friendly conversation with a lot of curiosity questions will help you clarify.

## THE CHALLENGE

You have a challenge. You can decide whether to influence or to control your teens, whether to raise their self-confidence (empower) or to run their lives (enable). You can focus either on building skills or on doing things for your teens to protect them. Parents often use the excuse that teens can make mistakes that could kill them or ruin their lives forever, but this is true at any age. Focusing on this fear invites parents to try to control their teens' lives rather than letting go so they can live their own lives.

Ask yourself, "Am I coming from fear or trust?" Trust gives your teen room to make mistakes and to learn from them. As Rudolph Dreikurs said, "Better a bruised knee than bruised courage. A broken knee can mend, but broken courage lasts forever."

### KIND AND FIRM PARENTING TOOLS TO REMEMBER

1. Enabling is doing for kids what they can do for themselves. It's intervening between them and life experience.
2. Kids can learn from the mistakes they make if parents don't stand between them and the consequences of their actions (life experience).
3. Empowering is giving kids a hand when they "fall down" because they made a mistake, or need a boost when they are working hard to help themselves.
4. Remind yourself that you are doing something when you use the methods described in this chapter. You don't have to punish or

control to be effective at reversing extremely negative patterns with your teen.

5. Prepare your teen for life by expanding on his or her inner resources.

6. Empowerment helps kids establish courage, confidence, resilience, responsibility, and a realistic attitude about life.

7. When dealing with teen issues, discover whether you can take small, medium, or bigger steps to empower instead of enabling your teen.

*Practical Application Activity*

Think back to when you were a teen. What was one of your hardest life lessons? Did your parents enable or empower you? What did they do? What was the outcome? What did you learn from the experience? How has that experience impacted your life? Your parenting?

# 10

## ARE YOU TEACHING
## LIFE SKILLS?

### BUILDING COMPETENCE AND A CAN-DO ATTITUDE

The more tools teens have, the better their lives work. Kids are quick studies, yet their ability to learn is often underutilized. Teens don't learn by being told what to do; they learn by being involved. They don't learn when parents do "to" or "for" them; they learn when parents engage "with" them. If you want your kids to have a can-do attitude as they go through life's challenges, it's not too late to teach life skills while they're still close enough to benefit from your encouragement—even though they may think they already know everything.

Look for teaching moments. Many opportunities arise for teaching life skills, such as those involving cars, money, clothing, shopping, family work, use of time, and attitudes toward learning and school.

Francine had been taking the responsibility to get her son Dan out of bed on Tuesday mornings for an early class. She would wake him up, he would go back to sleep. This scenario would continue, with increasing anger on both sides, until Francine would yank the covers off. Dan would then stumble out of bed, saying, "Get off my back," and finally leave about half an hour late. Francine received a letter from the teacher saying that if Dan missed one more time, he would fail the class.

Later, as Dan and his mother were driving alone in the car, she said, "I got a letter from your teacher today saying that if you miss one more class, you'll fail first period. Do you want to go to class tomorrow or do you want to miss it and fail the class?" Dan was quiet for a few seconds before saying, "I guess I'll go." Then his mother said, "Do you want me to help you get up, or do you want me to leave you alone?" He said, "Leave me alone."

She agreed and Dan said, "Thanks, Mom." (Quite a difference from, "Get off my back.") The next morning, Dan showered early and left on time. Mom was sure he could feel the difference in her manner—that she really meant what she said—that she really was turning this responsibility over to him. Kids seem to know when parents mean what they say and when they don't.

## PIGGYBACK ON YOUR TEEN'S INTERESTS

Some of the best teaching moments can be found when you *piggyback on your teens' interests*. For instance, most teenage girls are preoccupied with clothing. This preoccupation offers many opportunities to teach about budgeting, about earning money, and about planning ahead.

In Paula's family, the children received a clothing allowance twice a year. Paula decided to buy fewer but more expensive clothes. In her mind, she could always fill in her wardrobe by borrowing from friends and using her small monthly allowance.

Paula's mom insisted that new clothes were absolutely not to be loaned out or left on the floor. She was trying to prevent Paula from making mistakes, but then she remembered that she wanted to help Paula learn from her experience. She told her daughter, "Paula, I made a mistake. I wanted to protect you from losing these expensive clothes, but I'm sure you can figure out whether or not you want to loan your clothes. I know it's up to you to decide how you want to treat the clothes you have."

A few months later, Paula came to her mother in a rage. One of her friends had borrowed her designer jacket and lost it at a party. Mom bit her lip and skipped the "I told you so" lecture. She gave Paula a big hug and said, "I can see how upset you are. I'm so sorry." Paula looked at her mother and said, "I'll never let her borrow my clothes again." Teens can learn best, on their own, from making mistakes without shaming or blaming.

"Paula, would you be interested in an idea I have about loaning clothes?"

"Okay, Mom."

"You could tell your friends you want a deposit or something equally nice of theirs to hold until they return your clothing. This is called collateral."

"Thanks, Mom, but I don't think that would work with my friends. I'm just never going to let my friends borrow my nice stuff again. Their parents buy them whatever they want and they don't understand what it's like to be on a clothing allowance. I can't afford to lose my stuff."

"Good plan," replied Mom, as she hid her grin all the way into the other room.

## PLAN IN ADVANCE AND SCHEDULE TOGETHER

*Planning and scheduling together* is an excellent training method. Life is filled with arrangements that need to be made around busy schedules. If you are making all the plans yourself and then informing your teen, you are missing out on an excellent way to help him or her learn life skills and build character. Your children will have no idea from one minute to the next what is planned for them, and they in turn will expect you to do things for them, take them places, and even intervene and rescue them if they get too busy.

You'll get better results, show respect, and teach skills when you involve your teens in planning ahead, even if it takes more time. Put a calendar in a centrally located place so that everyone in the family can easily refer to it. You can use a family meeting for planning, too. At the meeting everyone can give their full attention to discussing upcoming activities and appointments. Everyone can then take part in planning ahead by noting what is happening, when it's happening, who needs to be involved, and who is responsible for what.

Although many people complain they don't have the time, they don't seem to count the time spent in chaos and frustration! Good planning eliminates these problems—but it still takes time, plus attention to details and cooperation.

Toni was getting ready to go back to high school for her junior year. She had mentioned to her parents the things she needed to do to prepare for school. After dinner one day, they sat at the table and made a list of what needed to be done. They got out the family calendar to figure out when each thing could be accomplished and which parent would be available to assist if needed. Toni worked out a budget with her folks for school clothes and an allowance that would cover the rising costs for school activities and personal expenses.

The family also figured out ways that Toni could get to school each day, as the school was too far for walking and the bus didn't run at the right times. This allowed Toni plenty of time to get on the phone and arrange carpools for the days when her folks couldn't take her.

Contrast this picture with Rick and Stephanie's situations where chaos and frustration reigned. Rick wanted to go to a hockey game to watch his favorite team. Because he didn't have a car or a license and the event was fifty miles away, he needed his parents' help to make the arrangements. Every time he asked them, they said they were busy and would talk about it later. Rick was frustrated—he wanted to know if he should save money to buy a ticket, and he wanted to have enough time to ask friends to go with him. Because Rick's parents didn't take him seriously, they didn't get back to him in time, and he missed the game. His parents didn't realize they were being rude and disrespectful; they just didn't see his plan as important as all the other things they were dealing with in their lives.

Rick's story isn't unusual. When Stephanie wanted to go to a dance, her parents weren't comfortable with her going out with a boy, so they kept putting off answering her questions about the dance. Stephanie couldn't make the arrangements all her friends were making—buying their dresses, planning where they would go to eat, arranging transportation—because her parents wouldn't respond, and she didn't know how to get through to them.

Both Rick and Stephanie ended up as adults with very few skills for planning ahead. They didn't think their opinions or needs were very important, so both ended up in relationships with people who took control. Had their parents understood more about taking the time to plan ahead and schedule together, Rick and Stephanie might have grown up with a completely different adult experience.

## CREATE A RUN-THROUGH REHEARSAL

On the morning of Tim's sixteenth birthday, he was first in line to get his driver's license. He passed his written test with a score of 97 and passed his behind-the-wheel driving test, which, in his mind, qualified him as an expert driver. He was ready to drive anything anywhere because the State of California said he could, and the state was bigger than his parents were!

When he came home, Tim asked his mother if he could drive her car into San Francisco.

Mom later told her friend Marcia about Tim's request. "We live in a small, quiet town. San Francisco is full of steep, scary hills and heavy traffic. It's a very big city. I told Tim, 'No. You just got your license an hour ago.' He said, 'But I've been waiting and dreaming of this moment. How can you ruin my life? The State of California says I'm ready to drive anywhere. They gave me a license. I got a 97 on the test. What's wrong with you? Do you hate me?' "

Marcia asked, "What are you going to do?"

"I have to say this honestly," Mom continued. "My car was my first thought. It's a really nice car, and I didn't want to see it all banged up. I was also concerned for Tim. I wanted to protect him. I was worried about him having trouble just getting on the ramp to the freeway! I pictured all kinds of disasters for him—on the freeway and on the hills in the city. But I really could see what his issues were. He felt like a grown-up finally. He had a license, he had freedom, he had power, he had wheels. Also, he loves San Francisco; we've taken many trips there as a family. Now he wants to go on his own and take his friends. How exciting for him!"

"Do you think he can handle it this soon?" Marcia asked.

"We're going to find a way to do this in small steps. Although he hates waiting, he understands that we can't always move at the pace he wants. We're going to dedicate the next two weekends to Tim, so he can take the whole family to San Francisco. We'll have him go places he would never go on his own, just to give him our own personal San Francisco driver's test, with lots of opportunities to park. We'll let him drive us everywhere—up and down hills, to North Beach, Fisherman's Wharf, Chinatown. After spending four days driving around San Francisco with him, I'll feel better and know firsthand that he can do it. Then I'm going to give him the keys to my car, tell him to have fun, and when he drives off, I'll call you and panic and cry. He'll gain a lot of confidence, and I'll have a closet heart attack."

Marcia laughed and said, "You always have had a flair for high drama."

Contrast this story with Lindy, whose mother discouraged her from going on the senior-class trip. Lindy's mother described how awful the trip would be. She said no one would have any fun unless they got drunk and slept around, and since Lindy wasn't that kind of person, she'd be happier staying home. Because Lindy didn't want to get drunk and sleep around—and because she had no reason to doubt her mother—she decided she wouldn't go.

When questioned, Lindy's mother said, "I've heard a lot of stories about this trip. I'm not sure if they're true, but if they are, I don't want my daughter to go. She can find some other way to celebrate graduation." But one thing she seemed to be ignoring was that in a few months Lindy would probably be living on her own at college. Not only would she lack the self-confidence that comes from handling difficult situations, she'd also lack the necessary skills—including decision making—because her mother made so many decisions for her.

This would have been a perfect opportunity for Lindy's mother to find some smaller steps her daughter could take so that she could practice uncomfortable social situations closer to home where her mom would be nearby to coach and dissect. Instead, Lindy, unnerved by her mother's fear, was scared to go out on her own.

Many teenagers want their parents to control them and to do things for them because they're afraid to grow up. If parents feed these teens' fears with fears of their own, their teenagers won't develop the skills necessary to become successful adults. Of course, there are also teens who refuse to be controlled and just plain rebel.

You can help your teens build courage by showing your enthusiasm for their growth process: "Won't it be exciting when you grow up and are old enough to leave home? Won't it be great when you get your first apartment? Aren't you looking forward to having your own cell-phone account?" Your enthusiasm will be contagious and will help them look forward to being grown-ups out in the world. More important, you can help teens be courageous by giving them the chance to learn from you step by step and then giving them the opportunity to use what they've learned.

One mother, who had conscientiously tried to provide her son with life skills, asked him if he thought all the grocery shopping and cooking he had done as a teen helped him as an adult. He replied, "Are you kidding? I don't know how I would be able to live like I do if I hadn't had all that help. I know how to shop for bargains, how to stretch my money, how to plan ahead. I know how to do menus! I know a lot of stuff."

## USE UNCONVENTIONAL APPROACHES LIKE TRICKS AND BETS

Kelly's grades were suffering. Her father, Pete, asked if she'd like to learn some tricks about studying. Kelly, feeling suspicious, asked, "What kinds of tricks?"

Her father replied, "I could teach you the 'handy-dandy four-step system' if you'd like."

Kelly's interest was piqued, so she asked, "Where did you learn this system?"

Her father explained that his friend Lissie told him about it to help him work on his own procrastination. He continued, "Kelly, it really helped me. Would you like to hear about it?"

Kelly said, "Okay."

### THE HANDY-DANDY FOUR-STEP SYSTEM

1. Decide what you want.
2. Make time for it.
3. Set up a deal or a trick to motivate yourself.
4. Use lists.

When Kelly asked how the four steps could help her, her father said that he would go through the steps with her if she would like. Kelly agreed.

First, Pete asked Kelly to think of some things that she really wanted to do each day. Kelly's list included spending time with friends, playing her guitar, studying, and watching TV.

For step two, Pete suggested that Kelly think of when she could make time for each of her choices. Kelly decided to be with her friends after school, and then come home and play her guitar, have dinner with the family, watch TV for thirty minutes, and then study.

Pete didn't point out that saving studying for last was doomed to fail. Instead, he went on to explain step three, making deals. He pointed out that people often don't do their least favorite things unless they first make deals with themselves. For example, "First I'll do what I don't like and get it over with," or, "First I'll do two things I like, then one thing I don't like, and save the best for last." He said another trick is to make dates with someone to do the things you don't like, explaining, "It can be more fun to study if you make a date to do it with someone else. And you usually won't disappoint a friend, even if you might be willing to let yourself down."

Finally, Pete showed Kelly how to make a list of her four interests that included the amount of time for each and any deals she made with herself. They talked about how easy it could be to go back to old habits and forget new plans when they weren't written down. Pete suggested that Kelly use the list as a way to remember the decisions she had made for herself.

Kelly wanted to know if her father planned to check up on her each day to see if she was following her list. Pete asked if that was what she wanted, and Kelly said, "No way!" So Pete said, "Good. My job is to help you learn. Your job is to decide if you want to use what you learn. I'll be happy to help if you ask me directly, but otherwise, it's up to you."

A friendly challenge can also help motivate teens to learn life skills. Deciding to try this method, Leilani said to her son, Jon, "I'll bet you can't get a B in that class."

Jon rose to the challenge, saying "How much?"

His mother challenged, "Ten dollars," and Jon agreed, "You're on!"

Since we don't advocate bribes, rewards, or taking away privileges, you may wonder how a bet is different. A bet can be used when a teen has said, "I could do it if I wanted to." To be effective, the bet must be made with a friendly, respectful, playful attitude. "You're telling me you can, but I've got money that says you can't. Are you willing to put your money where your mouth is?"

Parents can make bets with their teens without controlling them. But as soon as parents hold out a bribe or reward, they are trying to control them. The trick is to learn how to be helpful while avoiding control.

## LET YOUR TEENS TEACH YOU

One of the best ways to encourage and empower your teens is to let them teach you. They can teach you about their music, how to use smartphones, how to record TV shows, how to use a computer, and a million other things. If you're concerned about your teenager's driving habits, ask him or her to help you improve your own driving skills in as many ways as your teen thinks of. Or ask teens to share their hobbies with you, to show you how to sand a car, or to put on makeup so you can hardly see it's there. Your teens can be valuable resources if you give them the opportunity—and when you do, you not only demonstrate your respect for their abilities, but you also model the joys of learning.

When you're excited about learning new skills, you can help your teenagers see that learning benefits the learner. One teenager commented to her mother, "I just realized that the more I learn, the easier my life is." That's what raising teens is all about!

## USE ROUTINES

Most of the things you learned to do well started with a routine. Whatever you practice you get better at. The same goes for teens. Bad routines are easy to fall into; good routines take some thought and planning.

Instead of nagging her slightly overweight fourteen-year-old twins to get exercise, Jennifer challenged them to a weekly tennis match where she would play against both of them at the same time. The boys couldn't resist the challenge. After their mother beat them three weeks in a row, she asked the boys if they'd be interested in taking lessons, to which they happily agreed. She set them up with once-a-week lessons and continued to stick with the weekly challenge game. The boys decided they would practice one other time during the week on their own. After three months, the boys were beating Jennifer regularly, and they had also trimmed down considerably.

Josiah complained about being bullied at school. He was a skinny kid who never worked out, but instead spent hours at his computer. His dad asked him if he'd google information on martial arts classes in the area. Josiah said he'd do that, but he wasn't going to take classes. His dad said that was fine, but he'd like the information just the same, as he wondered if there was a difference between karate, aikido, kung fu, and jujitsu. Being the researcher that he was, Josiah started down the list, only to find that there were many more types of martial arts classes than he ever imagined. He came across a class on capoeira, a combination of martial arts, sports, and music, and started watching YouTube videos depicting the sport.

Josiah told his dad that even though he wasn't interested in taking a class, he might like to go to the capoeira class just to observe. His dad was happy to take him, and after the class, Josiah asked if he could sign up. His

dad said he would be willing to do that as long as Josiah agreed to take six classes before he quit. "Josiah," Dad said, "this sport looks really hard and I think it would be easy to get discouraged and give up before you start. I'm willing to invest the money in the class and the time to take you there if you're willing to tough it out for six weeks." By the time the six weeks were up, Josiah was sold and had created an exercise and learning habit that stuck with him throughout high school.

If your kids want to start something new, it's perfectly reasonable to expect them to commit to a certain number of classes before you invest in equipment or even disrupting your life to do a lot of driving. It's the repetition that makes a routine work. Don't insist that they stick with activities they don't like or that don't fit their personalities after their initial commitment.

## ENLIST THE HELP OF OTHERS TO PROVIDE INFORMATION TO YOUR TEENS

Often, teenagers are more willing to listen to someone else than they are to you. They may be motivated by other adults who serve as mentors and tutors.

If parents tell teens how great they are, they can write it off to the fact that the people complimenting them are their parents, but if someone else tells them, it usually sticks. If your teen is on a team, you probably don't have the same impact on him or her as does your teen's coach. If you and your kid fight about homework, that probably isn't going to happen with a tutor. Mentors and tutors can also help you. If a tutor asks you to back off, you might listen and agree to do that, but if your kid asks you to back off, you probably won't.

Kids who are involved in extracurricular activities or clubs outside of school or special interest classes have the opportunity to engage with many encouraging adults who leave lasting impressions on them. As a parent, you can encourage your kids to find activities they like and then spend the money to help them pursue these classes, trips, competitions, and so on. It's a worthwhile investment in your kids if you can swing it, along with driving them to practices and events and showing up for their performances and competitions when you can.

If you can keep your ego out of the way, you can be creative in helping your teens find other sources of learning.

Blythe was complaining about her parents to her friend's dad, Cal. She told Cal that her folks were way too strict and never listened. She said she hated the way they treated her like a baby, expecting her to come home by 9:00 p.m. when all her friends could come home at 10:00 p.m.

Cal listened as he always did and then said, "Blythe, I don't mean to sound trite, but being a parent of a teen isn't much easier than being a teen. Your folks are trying to do what they think is best and deal with their insecurities and fears."

"I know, I know, but I wish just once they could be reasonable."

"Well, Blythe," Cal said, "I'm sure you've already thought of this, but I wonder what would happen if you explained to them the reasons why it's important to you to stay out later and asked them to think about what you were saying before they interrupt. Maybe you could even suggest they call some of your friends' parents to hear about how other families handle curfew. Do you think you might find them a more willing audience?"

Blythe looked doubtful but said, "Thanks, Cal, I'll give it a try." Even if her parents still won't listen, Cal helped Blythe by sharing a perspective she probably didn't have. And he expressed it in a way she could hear and understand.

## MAKE IT A GAME

Making a game out of things can be a great way to teach skills. Buy a dictionary calendar and challenge your teens to learn new words and use them in sentences. Swap a joke a day with your teens. Play games like Scrabble or Pictionary. Now you can do many of these things on apps downloaded into your cell phones.

Other fun ways parents can teach skills to teens include asking them to survey other teens to find out how they and their families deal with money, curfews, allowances, and so on. Or help teens plan a party or a picnic. Once you decide to be creative, you'll find there are many ways to teach skills.

Embrace your job of teaching life skills, knowing that you are helping your teen build character. The time you spend now will pay big dividends down the road.

### KIND AND FIRM PARENTING TOOLS TO REMEMBER

1. To be effective teaching life skills to your teens, be sure they are involved. There's no way talking can compare with seeing and doing for building competence.
2. Knowing your teen's interests is the doorway to teaching life skills. Use your teen's interests as a natural way to hold his or her attention.
3. There's no better way to teach life skills than through a routine. Life is filled with routines, so why not work with your teen to set up some that work for both of you, instead of operating on the haphazard routines that may currently be running your family?

*Practical Application Activity*

Don't be afraid to learn new things yourself. Being a learner while your teen watches benefits both of you. No one likes being a beginner, but think of something you've been putting off learning and set it up. Talk about your fears, trials and tribulations, and successes, with your teen. Take an online class or workshops at the Apple store. Sign up for classes through Parks and Rec or the YMCA. Invite your teen to go with you or to come watch you learn.

# 11

# HOW WIRED ARE YOUR TEENS?

## THE INTERNET AND OTHER ELECTRONIC CHALLENGES

P arents of teens are now facing challenges unheard of a few years ago—how to deal with the Internet, social networks, cell phones, texting, sexting, cyberbullying, reality TV shows, and gaming. Before this book goes to print, there will probably be several more updates to media and technology. You'll find tools in this chapter for dealing with present and future electronic challenges. (Much of the research for this chapter was conducted over the Internet.) In additon to Positive Discipline tools, you'll find hundreds of helpful websites that can give you added assistance for dealing with these challenges. Just google "teens and technology."

Our guess is that some of you grew up without PlayStations, Nintendos, Xboxes, Roku, video games, cell phones, personal computers, the Internet, or Internet chat rooms. You probably did not have MySpace or

Facebook and reality TV. Times have changed, and if you are parenting a teen, you have to figure out how to deal with all this "new stuff."

What we mean by "new stuff" are those things that have become prevalent since you were a teen. Reality TV seems to be more popular every year. According to a news release in 2009, the word "sexting" didn't exist two years earlier. WikiAnswers states, "Cyberbullying quite simply started when the Internet became a common tool for anonymous users to say what they please without thinking of the consequences to the other anonymous users on the Internet." So really, cyberbullying most likely started in the mid-1990s. In 1999, only twenty-three blogs were listed. By 2000, more than three hundred blogs a day were started. Recently someone commented that blogs were obsolete. (A lot of bloggers might find that comment ridiculous, but it is an indication of how quickly things can change.) Maybe it is because Twitter takes less time.

In the fairly recent past, children of all ages didn't have cell phones or do most of their communicating through text messaging. Most families didn't have more than one computer in their homes along with computer games for both individual and group entertainment. Nor were all kids given or expected to have a computer for their own to use at school as is required by many schools today. Toddlers didn't know how to use iPads or play games or read books or watch movies on them. Today, go to any restaurant and count how many toddlers are glued to someone's iPhone.

Here's what hasn't changed—the struggle between teens and their parents has stayed very much the same, as have the methods for dealing with such drastic changes. We see the use of punishment and control, fear-based parenting, lectures, rewards and threats, spoiling, or even permissiveness sprinkled with "teens will be teens."

## INTERNET AND SOCIAL NETWORKS: ASSET OR LIABILITY?

Our grandkids are more comfortable with computers by age two than we are after using them for years. The two-year-olds (and younger) can work our cell phones, iPods, iPads, and computer games with ease. They can find their way to YouTube or Angry Birds without batting an eye. They don't feel discouraged learning how to use media the way we do. Either it works or it doesn't, and when it doesn't, there is no scolding, humiliating, shaming, or blaming from the electronic device. It's just an encouraging implication to try again until they get it or to ask for help from a sibling or friend or a parent.

Your teens may be listening to music, watching videos, playing video games, or going to movies that promote death, destruction, violence, disrespect for men and women, and worse. They may have hard-core porn hidden under the mattress or sexist posters hanging in their rooms. They may visit websites that show explicit sexual activities. What's a parent to do?

Within the boundaries of your values, you may wish to allow your children to experience some or all of the above, or you may wish to prohibit them from doing so. If you choose prohibition, recognize that many teens are motivated by forbidden fruit, so you'll have to use persuasion and advocacy rather than arbitrary or dogmatic denial.

We realize that there are adults who see these devices as the devil's spawn, but we don't judge the device or think they are the bad guys. We encourage you to understand their possibilities and work with your kids to use them safely and respectfully and in a balanced way—and even teach values and life skills. Electronics can be entertaining, informative, and help kids develop many transferable skills when used with awareness. It is overuse and inappropriate use that create serious problems. The real trick is to get children involved in creating healthy guidelines for the use of electronic equipment.

## SUGGESTIONS FOR SETTING UP GUIDELINES

1. Give kids limited choices about how long or when they can use media. For example: thirty minutes to one hour (not related to homework) on school nights; ninety minutes to two hours on weekends.
2. Don't put TV sets or computers in your kids' rooms.

3. Decide together on a nighttime "parking lot" for all electronics from 10:00 p.m to 6:00 a.m.—maybe in the garage. (Some teens are texting all hours of the night and then wonder why they feel so tired and cranky the next day.)

4. Establish a "parents' library" where all electronics are stored and checked out for limited time periods.

5. Talk with the kids about what they are watching or doing or playing.

6. Don't spend a fortune on computer games and downloads and apps if you aren't comfortable with your kids using them. Get the kids involved in earning and paying for these things. Do *not* give your teens your iTunes password.

7. Model a balanced life instead of being glued to a screen yourself.

8. If there are sites off-limits, discuss these with your kids and let them know why you think they should be off-limits. Listen to your kids' opinions about them. Negotiate if needed.

9. If some sites or shows or games are questionable, schedule them when you can sit next to the kids and view or use them together so you can have a running dialogue about them.

10. Let the kids know that if you think their behavior is addictive, you'll ban media time until they can figure out how to limit their use.

11. Let the kids know they need to set up a rotation for sharing equipment, games, and so on.

12. Set up media-free zones, such as one day per week or month that is media free. No media during meals. Talk with your kids instead.

13. Don't expect kids to follow media agreements when you aren't home to monitor them. If you think the kids are abusing agreements, confiscate equipment and allow it to be used only when you're around to monitor.

14. It is not your child's birthright to have electronic equipment. A lot of discussion needs to happen before adding a new piece of equipment to the family, including how it will be paid for, used, shared, and maintained. It is always okay for you to say no.

15. You may need to set up plans with prepaid services that shut the equipment off if it is overused. Or you can have your kids save in advance to pay for part of the usage service rather than advancing them money and expecting them to repay you.

16. Use headsets whenever appropriate to limit the noise levels from electronics in your home. Headsets are especially crucial with cell phones until further research proves that cell phones *don't* cause brain tumors from the radiation emitted.

17. Have the kids report on school policy for use of electronic devices—or check it out yourself.

18. Make sure all cars are equipped with hands-free equipment if your kids have cell phones. Let the kids know that people have been killed by drivers texting while driving, and that your teen will immediately lose priveleges for cell-phone use if he or she is found texting and driving. When instituting such an extreme measure, make sure your teens are given the opportunity to figure out a way that they can prove to you that they can try again. Make it their responsibility to come up with the solution that you believe will work.

19. Don't underestimate the creativity and ingenuity of your kids if you are considering adding tracking features to their cell phones. You could be spending a lot of extra money to know where your child is—while the cell phone may be parked somewhere else.

20. Go to http://www.netsmartz.org/Parents for workshops, help, and ideas for managing teens and media.

## ADVICE FROM A COMPUTER-SAVVY DAD

Jane's son Ken Ainge had some great advice for monitoring a household of teens and their electronic devices. When asking Ken how he managed being the computer tech that he is, here's what he said: "I am totally and completely involved in anything they do. I subscribe to SMS feeds, so anytime they tweet, I get a copy. I know how the kids are doing and feeling from being involved with their MySpace, Facebook, and Tumblr sites. I know all their passwords and they know it. It's not as if the Internet is private. It's not, so since the rest of the world can be watching, so can I. We watch shows together on *20/20* and TV about the Internet and cybercrime.

"If anyone is using one of my kids' phones to harass or bully them, they can choose to change their phone number or I'll change it for them. There have been times where I had to take their phone, because they were getting too upset and too involved in the negativity that was coming their way. I told them the phone was going to have a time-out because they were getting too upset, and that when things calmed down and they calmed down, I'd give their phones back.

"Another thing I do is use the app Find my iPhone so I know were their phones are. Some plans call it 'the family locate.' I present it as a safety issue so I know where they are."

Sounds like Ken has a lot of trust with his kids and that they see his help as supportive. They know they won't get in trouble, so they're very open and accepting of his efforts to keep them safe. Keep in mind, however, that what works for one family and set of teens may not be the agreement that works for another, and the values driving Positive Discipline aren't suddenly suspended when a computer is involved. For many teens, parents monitoring 100 percent of their online activity is going to be seen as no different from parents monitoring 100 percent of their real-life activity—and could easily result in the same type of resentment and power struggles. Parents need to remember that the same basic principles of trust and respect apply online as apply in real life, and attempts at controlling their teen's every move is unlikely to solve anything. Parents and teens need to negotiate online space the same way they would in real life, including honest dialogue and a willingness on the part of the parents to respect their teen's need for privacy and independence while still being supportive.

## SOMETIMES EXTREME INTERVENTIONS ARE NEEDED

Thirteen-year-old Kirk was addicted to his computer. He spent every waking hour when not in school sitting in front of his computer, playing games or surfing the Internet (an activity that many adults find just as addicting). Kirk's parents tried working on solutions with  him, but nothing worked. His parents finally became very firm yet still kind. During summer vacation, they told Kirk that from then on he would not be able to use the computer between noon and 6:00 p.m. Kirk's mom told him that they would eat lunch together and would then spend an hour doing something together, such as visiting the library, going for a bike ride, or playing a board game. They could decide on this activity together. From 2:00 to 6:00 p.m., it would be up to Kirk to decide what he wanted to do with his time—but the computer was off-limits. Kirk complained and whined. At first he sat listlessly in a chair, not doing anything; but soon he was going through his room looking for something new to do. He even decided to read the books his teacher had recommended for summer reading. After a week, he stopped pouting and engaged in small talk with his mom over toasted cheese sandwiches he prepared for lunch.

This example illustrates that it is the parent's job to be firm as well as kind. Had Kirk been able to work out a solution on his own, his parents would have been happy to let him. What wasn't okay was to let the problem continue.

## SOCIAL NETWORKS, YOUTUBE, AND OTHER INTERNET OPTIONS

When we were teens, we socialized in the neighborhood, playing kick the can and red light green light. We played in each other's rooms or at the park or neighborhood skating rink. When our kids were teens, they would socialize with their friends at school and then come home and talk on the phone with them. Or they would ask us to drive them to their friends or invite their friends over to hang out.

Now when kids socialize, they head to their computer and MySpace, Facebook, Tumblr, and more, or they send hundreds of text messages through their cell phones. They still socialize at school or parties or sporting events or teams or practices or classes, but it is truly a different world, and not necessarily a worse one. The trick is to help your teens create some balance in their lives. That may be difficult, because their idea of balance is probably different from yours, and on top of that, you probably don't have a lot of balance in your life either and may not know how to help them create some.

The simplest way to create balance is to use the calendar to schedule activities. Include media-free times, family dinners, family outings, sporting events, classes (yoga, tai chi, dance, etc.). Creating balance can be challenging for families that have kids of different ages, or single parents, or two working parents, but it can be done with some planning and follow-through.

We suggest you research how to help keep teens safe when they are social networking on the Internet. If you don't know how to do this research, ask your kids for help or do it with them. Remind your kids often that the Internet isn't private and that the person responding to them on a social network site could easily be a fifty-year-old-guy posing as a fifteen-year-old teenager. Your kids shouldn't assume people are who they claim to be.

Visit your kids on their social network sites. Many parents let the kids know that they can have an Internet presence as long as the parents can also access the sites and that parents and teens can talk about what is going on. Make it a point to know who your teens are talking to. One dad even contacted the parents of one of the kids on his daughter's Facebook who was harassing his daughter. He told the parents what was going on and asked if they would please talk to their son. They were shocked and had no idea of what was going on, and they were glad to talk with their son.

If you think your teen is being bullied or sending out sexually explicit pictures or messages (sexting), talk with him or her, letting your teen know you're there to help and that he or she doesn't have to deal with the problem alone.

If you think the kids are sacrificing schoolwork because of time on the Internet, disable or remove the equipment until the kids catch up in school. Or ask your kids for suggestions and be willing to try them out for a week at a time. If they need the computer to research schoolwork, keep the power cords under lock and key and expect the kids to check them out while you are home so you can monitor the use. You can ask the kids for collateral that you will hold until they return the power cord. This could be a favorite item of clothing or jewelry or a cell phone or iPod, and so on.

We are impressed by some of the things teens do on the Internet. A fourteen-year-old who was failing English designed the most beautiful Facebook page without any spelling errors, filled with quotes from the books assigned that she was supposed to be reading. A twelve-year-old diagnosed with ADHD, and incapable of focusing in the classroom, spent hours and hours filming himself and his friends doing tricks on a skateboard and bicycle and then uploading them to YouTube with musical accompaniment. A young boy (around thirteen) played a computer game with other players throughout the world. Most didn't speak English, but they communicated through the game. Several players thought the thirteen-year-old was in his twenties or thirties and were shocked to find out he was only thirteen because he was so intelligent and capable. Another young man spends hours building architectural structures on the computer. We're sure he's in training for a career as an architect. He'll be ahead of the game once he starts college due to all his experience that is sheer "play" to him now. Another young man who spent hours playing driving/racing computer games now works for a large company designing motorcycles.

Many parents think what we've described is a waste of time and a distraction from schoolwork. It could be, but it also could be early training and skill development for future successes. So many jobs require comfort and competence with computers, and the kids who are using them as teens certainly have a jump start. Those of us who came to computers later in life will never have the skills or ease of use that kids who started early have. Recently one of the author's twenty-seven-year-old nephews, who works in a high-paying professional job involving advanced computer skills, said, "I'm a dinosaur on the computer compared to the new guys joining the company. The new guys have had handhelds since they were babies and there's no way to keep up with them." His twenty-two-year-old cousin talked with great excitement about law school where she specializes in intellectual property. She'll be working in a groundbreaking field, one that wouldn't be open to her if she hadn't spent so many years as a kid on the computer.

## INTERNET SCHOOL

A number of online high school programs are available, some of them free, for kids who have decided that attending school isn't for them. A quick search of the Internet will help you and your teen learn about online high schools that offer programs built around each student's goals, needs, and learning style. Students get to enjoy an individualized high school experience in an online environment that offers extensive courses taught by certified teachers and ends with getting a diploma recognized by colleges and universities nationwide. In the past, too many of these kids ended up as high school dropouts. Now they have the opportunity to be engaged, challenged, and successful.

## REALITY TV

We've already covered many suggestions for TV viewing, and they apply here as well. In addition, feel free to use parental controls and set them to the level you are comfortable with. A single dad described how he and his twelve-year-old daughter watch *The Bachelor* and *The Bachelorette* and laugh together and discuss everything they see. They talk about how silly some of the contestants act, and how often they don't show respect for themselves or others. His daughter is especially interested because he's single. She's learning a lot about dating from the conversations they have as they watch the show. If you're in doubt, watch the show first before you watch it with your teen to make sure it's a show you feel comfortable with. You know your teens and what they can handle.

You may get a lot of pressure from your teens who say that all their friends get to watch certain TV shows, so why can't they? You know you don't have to give in to that pressure, but it would certainly be appropriate to let your child know that you'll watch the show first and then have a conversation about it, including if and when he or she can watch the show. It's always best to have a dialogue with your teen instead of a mandate.

Every generation's parents have their challenges. The ideas in this book will help you deal with the challenges of the day, and maybe even get to know your teen better. Who knows, it might also help you become more savvy about what technology has to offer *you*. In addition to being difficult and annoying, teens can also be our teachers and our motivators. Admit it, who do you ask to set your watch or help you upload a picture or figure out how to download music onto your iPod? By the time your teens grow up and move away, hopefully you've been a good student, because if you haven't, you'll have to start paying for those services.

## KIND AND FIRM PARENTING TOOLS TO REMEMBER

1. Even though the electronic world is changing at light speed, parents are slow to upgrade their methods for dealing with teens' use of technology. There is a lot of help for you on the Internet to deal effectively with the advances in electronics.

2. You can choose to look at the advent of electronics as an asset or a liability. Your teens are already behind in this world if you've prevented them from being involved in the electronic world. It's not the item that is good or evil but how it is used that makes the

difference. Be open-minded, and keep in mind that your child will be living in a different world than the one you grew up in and may benefit greatly from using electronics at a young age.

3. Work with your kids to establish guidelines for using electronics.

4. Remind your kids that the Internet is a public highway and that anyone can be viewing their posts. Let them know that you will be doing the same.

5. Learning on the computer is very nonjudgmental, which means that some of your kids will do better with computer courses than they can in a traditional school. Be open to possibilities.

### *Practical Application Activity*

Make a list of the advances in science since you were a kid, and after each item, write a few words as to how this advance has affected your life. Has it been a positive or a negative experience? Share your list with your kids and ask them to do the same with you.

# 12

# WHY DO THEY ACT LIKE THAT?

## TEEN PSYCHOLOGY

When a teen skips classes, fights with his siblings, keeps his backpack like a garbage can, "forgets" his homework, and takes a sudden behavioral dive into sullenness and avoidance one minute and extreme agitation the next, it's typical for some to start diagnosing, looking for a disease. A typical diagnosis is "ODD" (oppositional defiant disorder). (It is interesting to us that the more "controlling" a parent is, the more "defiant" some teens become.) If you watch enough television, you're probably familiar with the many "diagnoses" and pills to treat them. If you go to the doctor, you may get confirmation that your diagnosis is correct. This is called a "disease model" and is extremely popular today.

We explain behavior differently. We look for discouraged thinking instead of a disease. Then we apply an encouragement model of "treatment" that helps both you and your teen feel better and do better.

In our work with parents of teens, we've discovered that some behaviors are scarier than others. Often these behaviors send you or your teen to someone who can prescribe medication. Over the years, we've seen the treatments that rely heavily on medications become scarier than the behaviors. Fortunately, there are now studies that support our belief that kids are being dangerously overmedicated (http://ideas .time.com/2011/12/02/bromides-are-no-better-than -zyprexa/). The information in this chapter will help you deal with challenging behaviors without medication. More detailed information on scary behavior is in the next chapter.

## A LITTLE BIT OF PSYCHOLOGY CAN GO A LONG WAY

Adlerian therapists use early memories and other techniques to help them understand the private logic of their clients. Their focus is on understanding the perceptions, beliefs, private logic, or separate reality that inspires the behavior or point of view of each individual.

We are students of the psychology of Alfred Adler and Rudolf Dreikurs, the fathers of modern psychology. Adler (1870–1937) had radically different thinking about human nature and motivation than his contemporaries. He and his colleague, Rudolf Dreikurs, embraced concepts of social equality, mutual respect, encouragement, holism, and human potential. They engineered ideas and techniques that are now familiar to practitioners everywhere, although they are rarely credited.

As parents, you don't have to be trained psychologists, but it does help to know how to tap into the separate realities of your teens. In fact, without this information, all you have are assumptions. When you act on those assumptions, they may have nothing to do with why your teens behave the way they do. Our goal is to help you see that a little bit of psychological understanding can go a long way to help you parent your teens. Think of this chapter as an introduction to adolescent psychology and open your mind and your heart as you learn about why teens do what they do.

## BEHAVIOR IS MOTIVATED BY AN INDIVIDUAL'S PERCEPTION

To find out the hidden thoughts that drive behavior, ask your teens for some memories of when they were kids. When they tell you their memories, don't correct them or say it didn't happen that way. Do ask how they felt when the "incident" happened. Think of the memory as a story with hidden information that explains why people do what they do.

Thirteen-year-old Kevin was extremely aggressive to his younger brother, bullying kids at school, getting the worst grades of his life, and getting in constant trouble. In spite of all the help and parental interventions, he seemed to be showing the world that no one could make him

do anything, that he was unlovable, awful to be around, and that he hated everything and everybody. His teachers tried to get him to comply by using rewards, punishments, removal from class, threats of expulsion, and calls to his parents. His parents tried to help him by using patience, anger, threats, praise, ignoring, and shaming. Nothing seemed to work. The adults were sure he had some kind of genetic, inherited problem—maybe one of those chemical imbalances so often talked about in the news. Maybe he was depressed and needed to be put on antidepressants. Or maybe he had ODD or was bipolar.

Everyone was dealing with Kevin based on their perceptions of him, but no one thought to find out about Kevin's perceptions—how he thought and how he felt. There were many reasons that no one thought about Kevin's feelings: adults rarely think that children have different perceptions than they do; the conventional wisdom says that problems are genetic or inherited and are some sort of disease; most people don't have a true understanding of how personality is formed; and everyone knows that adolescents, especially boys, can be very aggressive and difficult. The discipline style of parents and teachers also plays a part. However, the challenges his parents and teachers had with Kevin were not caused by a disease or a chemical imbalance and didn't require drugs. They had more to do with Kevin's perceptions of himself and his beliefs about how to manage his world.

After attending a Positive Discipline parenting class, his parents decided to try deciphering the *code* of Kevin's behavior (which was formed at a subconscious level) by trying some of the suggested methods. To help Kevin discover his perceptions of himself, they asked Kevin if he could remember things from when he was a little kid.

Kevin remembered when he was about four years old. He was playing with his sister (who was about ten at the time) and a kid in the neighborhood. The neighbor kid put some cleaning solution in a glass and tried to get Kevin to drink it. Kevin's sister knew the solution was poisonous and could hurt him, so she screamed and knocked the glass out of the kid's hand.

His parents asked Kevin for a feeling word to describe how he felt when this happened and he replied, "Angry." Surprised, they asked him why he was angry that his sister tried to save his life. Kevin responded that nothing ever happened to the kid who tried to kill him, so he decided (at age four) that nobody really cared about him and that he would be better off dead. This perception became the underlying theme in Kevin's life, motivating most of his behavior. Kevin didn't consciously know that this belief was driving his behavior, but the memory work helped bring to the surface a very powerful force that was now operating in the background of his relationships.

It is important to understand that when dealing with human behavior, the "truth" or commonsense logic of a situation does not matter. Rather, as with Kevin, all behavior is motivated by each individual's perception of what is true. Prescribing drugs does not change perceptions; instead, it often makes the situation worse.

It is the nature of human beings to look for evidence to support their early beliefs, and they can distort just about any situation to fit what they believe. In addition, drugs not only make the situation worse, they have side effects. When people take pills to control behavior, often their thinking becomes more distorted, their feelings become more extreme or numb, and their behaviors become more dangerous. Mix these reactions with adolescent hormones and brain development, or drugs that teens might be secretly using, and the result is a volatile situation just waiting to explode into some kind of personal or public tragedy.

Kevin's parents told him they were so sorry that his feelings were hurt and told him they loved him and were so glad that he was in the family. Kevin countered with, "I wish I were a dog, because everybody would like having me around and they'd pet me and play with me." Surprisingly, this information had an immediate positive effect on Kevin's parents. Instead of feeling afraid, angered, challenged, or disgusted with Kevin, they were able to tap into his feelings of isolation, hurt, and abandonment. They began to cuddle him (yes, even though he was thirteen, Kevin still liked being hugged), to spend fun time with him, and to listen to his complaints of injustice. They didn't argue or try to change his mind. Kevin's behavior changed dramatically. He stopped hitting his younger brother. He stopped fighting with his parents about going to school. His relationships with his teachers and his grades improved. Instead of acting disdainful at family meetings, he became very clever about finding helpful solutions to problems that were put on the agenda.

## THINK, FEEL, DO

Unconscious thoughts lead to behavior by creating feelings that provide the fuel for actions. This piece of information is so important that we'll say it in another way. Thoughts create feelings, and feelings create actions; and all this happens automatically until we learn to recognize the pattern and change it. We call this "think, feel, do." The following scenarios, from interviews with a group of teens, show teens' thoughts, decisions (that have become beliefs), and resulting feelings and actions of those beliefs.

### Sixteen-Year-Old Boy

*Event*: Parents' sudden divorce

*Teen's Decision*: My parents aren't the perfect people I thought they were. I had them on a pedestal, and they both disappointed me. I can't count on them now; I can only count on myself.

*Teen's Feelings*: Anger, betrayal, loss, fear

*Teen's Behavior*: To stop living like a beer-drinking airhead and to take charge of his life

In the same situation, another teen might come to a totally different conclusion such as: Now that my family is wrecked, I might as well go party.

### Thirteen-Year-Old Girl

*Event*: Parents' attempt to set up a financial reward system for good grades to motivate daughter to improve on D's and F's

*Teen's Decision*: All my parents care about is whether I go to college. They don't like me unless I'm how they want me to be. They don't even know or care about the things that are important to me.

*Teen's Feelings*: Anger, hurt

*Teen's Behavior*: To get revenge on parents by running away or by doing other things to hurt them, including hurting herself by cutting into her arms with a knife

### Fifteen-Year-Old Boy

*Event*: Childhood friend's death from illness

*Teen's Decision*: I'll never make another friend because I don't ever want to feel this kind of pain again.

*Teen's Feelings*: Grief, despair, hopelessness

*Teen's Behavior*: When his family moved to a new community shortly after the death of his friend, he decided the only way to honor his commitment to himself was not to make any new friends and to flunk out of school.

### Thirteen-Year-Old Girl

*Event*: Parents' constant fighting and cold war

*Teen's Decision*: My parents are probably going to get a divorce because they're so mean to each other. If they do divorce, they'll probably split up the family, and one parent will take me and the other will keep my brother. They'll probably move far away from each other, and I'll never get to see my brother again.

*Teen's Feelings*: Hurt, fear

*Teen's Behavior*: Noticing that her brother could make his mother really angry by refusing to do chores, she decided to copy him so her mother would let both kids live with their father. That way, at least she wouldn't be separated from her brother. Therefore, she refused to do any of the chores she had agreed to do.

Behavior always makes sense when you understand perceptions and private logic. For this reason, it was impossible to refocus the preceding teens before understanding the beliefs and feelings motivating their behavior. Lumping them into a group of kids who have no impulse control and don't think for themselves might feel comforting to some adults, but it certainly doesn't get to the bottom of the issues.

Understanding how your teens really think and feel takes a nonjudgmental attitude and the ability to keep your own perceptions separate. Teenagers place a tremendous amount of trust in the people to whom they confide their private thoughts and feelings. Sometimes the help of a therapist is the only way to get at a teen's innermost beliefs. But whoever elicits a teen's confidence must treat it with the utmost respect and seriousness; otherwise, the teen will feel betrayed as a result of sharing his or her private world.

The words of a teen giving input for this revision illustrate how important it is to know what your kids really think. She said, "What a lot of parents don't realize is that by understanding their teen more, it opens their teen's ears so they can return the favor. Parents could really learn a lot from their teens. Don't throw so many questions at a teen at once; it drives us insane. Find a way to calmly let us know what you want to know whenever we are going out, and eventually we'll start letting you know without the billions of questions that put us on the spot. Teens are going to do what they're going to do whether you tell us to or not. I like the phrase, 'I wish you would . . .' that is recommended in this book. Parents should let their teens know that they aren't expected to always make the right choices, but whatever choices they do make, whether they are good or bad, they will have to face the consequences. Some teens don't always learn from their mistakes the first time, so don't always expect them to. Parents also need to remember that childhood only comes once! We aren't ever going to get these times back, so lighten up, let us be kids and have fun! But guide us; don't let us ruin it for ourselves. We may not always seem like we're listening, but we are. So relax."

## YOUR TEEN'S SLICE OF THE "FAMILY PIE" EXPLAINS A LOT ABOUT BEHAVIOR

Children in a family use their own private logic to decide what they need to do to achieve their primary goals of belonging and significance. When you were growing up, your personality was strongly influenced by the sibling you saw as your chief competitor—although you didn't consciously realize this. Your children do the same.

They seem to believe that only one sibling can be special in a certain way; if one sibling has already decided to find belonging and significance by being the "good" child, another may decide to be the "social" child, the "athletic" child, the "shy" child, or the "rebel." We call these choices "slices of the family pie."

The family pie is composed of the children in

the family, but not the parents. If a child is an only child, he or she gets the whole family pie, but may compare him- or herself with the same-sex parent, a kid in the neighborhood, a cousin, or a sibling who has died. When asked who their chief competitor was, most only children are quick to name a specific person.

Many oldest children feel they must always be first; they become competitive overachievers. Second children often become the "we try harder" kids, peacemakers, or the rebels. If kids end up being middle children, they constantly find themselves in the middle as mediators or problem solvers, or they may walk around with a chip on their shoulder, thinking they are invisible. The youngest become the adorable ones, used to having things done for them; they often develop skills for manipulating others to take care of them. Other youngest children become competitive, wanting everything their older siblings have; often these youngest feel they aren't good enough or smart enough because they can't do what the big kids can do. Only children like to be special and often compare themselves with adults; sometimes this leads to feelings of inadequacy, because everyone else seems more capable than they are.

Many of the problems that parents deal with during their children's teen years have their origin in the family pie. You can better understand the private logic of your teenagers when you know what slice of the family pie they have chosen.

## THE NO-PROBLEM KID

In one family, the eldest boy consistently stated that he didn't have any problems; he never lost the opportunity to point out that his sister was the problem child in their family. The slice of the family pie he had chosen was to be perfect. He was trying to be special and different in the family by "having no problems." Convinced that if he revealed a problem, it would make him the "bad, sick" boy, he found it hard to get help with anything. He was also trapped in the cycle of trying to be perfect at all times. If he couldn't be perfect all the time, at the least he would find a way to show everyone how imperfect his sister was.

The parents inadvertently played into fortifying the teen's beliefs, often complimenting him for being easier to be around than his difficult sister or blaming her for problems, insisting she was the instigator. To encourage both kids, the parents need to learn to stress the uniqueness of each kid in positive ways, to put the kids in the same boat when they are arguing, and to stress the importance of mistakes as opportunities to learn as opposed to something to be ashamed of. The family did a lot of role-playing at their family meetings with the parents playing the parts of the kids and the kids playing the parents. Everyone learned a lot through role-playing, especially when they were able to identify what they were thinking, feeling, and deciding as they played the other person. We highly recommend that you do the same with your family to increase empathy and understanding.

## MISTAKEN GOALS OF BEHAVIOR ARE BASED ON UNDERLYING BELIEFS

Rudolf Dreikurs identified what he called "four mistaken goals (or purposes) of behavior": to get attention or special service, to have power over others, to seek justice through revenge, or to be left alone without anyone expecting anything of them (called "assumed inadequacy"). Some recent Adlerian psychologists have added a fifth goal for teens, which is to seek excitement.

They are called "mistaken goals" because children mistakenly believe that the only way to find belonging and significance is through behaviors that often achieve the opposite of what they really want. Instead of achieving their goal of belonging, they find alienation from those closest to them, as well as deeper discouragement. Their mistaken goal becomes a vicious cycle: the more discouraged they become, the more they escalate their efforts through the mistaken goal.

Behavior has a purpose, even though a teen may not be aware of the purpose of his or her behavior. When you deal with your teen's behavior without understanding and addressing the underlying beliefs, you will be frustrated in your efforts to effect change. Becoming aware of mistaken goals can help you understand your teens, improve your relationship with them, and help them see options for their behavior. The four mistaken goals each have a corresponding mistaken belief, as shown in the following chart.

## MISTAKEN GOALS

| The Child's Goal Is | If the Parent/ Teacher Feels | And Tends to React by | And if the Child's Response Is | The Belief Behind the Child's Behavior Is | Coded Messages | Parent/Teacher Proactive and Empowering Responses Include |
|---|---|---|---|---|---|---|
| **Undue Attention** (to keep others busy or to get special service) | Annoyed Irritated Worried Guilty | Reminding Coaxing Doing things for the child he/she could do for him/herself | Stops temporarily, but later resumes same or another disturbing behavior | I count (belong) only when I'm being noticed or getting special service. I'm only important when I'm keeping you busy with me. | **Notice Me. Involve Me Usefully.** | Redirect by involving child in a useful task to gain useful attention; ignore (touch without words); say what you will do, ("I love you and __," (i.e., I love/care about you and will spend time with you later."); Avoid special service; have faith in child to deal with feelings (don't fix or rescue); plan special time; help child create routine charts; engage child in problem-solving; use family/class meetings; set up nonverbal signals; ignore behavior with hand on shoulder. |
| **Misguided Power** (to be boss) | Angry Challenged Threatened Defeated | Fighting Giving in Thinking, "You can't get away with it" or "I'll make you." Wanting to be right. | Intensifies behavior. Complies with defiance. Feels he/she's won when parent/ teacher is upset even if he/she has to comply. Passive power (says yes but doesn't follow through). | I belong only when I'm boss, in control, or proving no one can boss me. You can't make me. | **Let Me Help. Give Me Choices.** | Redirect to positive power by asking for help; offer limited choices; don't fight and don't give in; withdraw from conflict; be firm and kind; act, don't talk; decide what you will do; let routines be the boss; leave and calm down; develop mutual respect; set a few reasonable limits; practice follow-through; use family/class meetings. |

| Revenge (to get even) | Hurt Disappointed Disbelieving Disgusted | Hurting back Shaming Thinking, "How could you do such a thing?" | Retaliates Intensifies Escalates the same behavior or chooses another weapon | I don't think I belong so I'll hurt others as I feel hurt. I can't be liked or loved. | **I'm Hurting. Validate My Feelings.** | Acknowledge hurt feelings; avoid feeling hurt; avoid punishment and retaliation; build trust; use reflective listening; share your feelings; make amends; show you care; act, don't talk; encourage strengths; put kids in same boat (don't take sides); use family/class meetings. |
|---|---|---|---|---|---|---|
| **Assumed Inadequacy** (to give up and be left alone) | Despair Hopeless Helpless Inadequate | Giving up Doing things for the child that he/she could do for him/herself Over-helping | Retreats further Becomes passive Shows no improvement Is not responsive | I can't belong because I'm not perfect, so I'll convince others not to expect anything of me; I am helpless and unable; it's no use trying because I won't do it right. | **Don't Give Up On Me. Show Me A Small Step.** | Break down task into small steps; stop all criticism; encourage any positive attempt; have faith in child's abilities; focus on assets; don't pity; don't give up; set up opportunities for success; teach skills/show how, but don't do for; enjoy the child; build on his/her interests; use family/class meetings. |

## MISTAKEN GOALS AND THEIR UNDERLYING BELIEFS

1. Undue Attention/Special Service: "I am significant when you notice me and treat me special, and do things for me I could do for myself." Everyone wants recognition and attention. The problem occurs when attention and recognition are sought through behaviors that are annoying ("Look at me, look at me") instead of respectful ("I feel special when I am making a contribution or helping others feel special"). To understand what your teens need, imagine them wearing a T-shirt with the coded message that says, "Notice me. Involve me usefully."

2. **Misguided Power:** "I am significant when I do what I want—or at least don't do what you want."

   Everyone wants power and will use their power, either in contributing ways or in destructive ways. When parents try to control teens, teens are likely to respond by using their power in rebellious ways. What teens need are guidance and the skills to learn how to use their power in constructive ways. To help your teens with this, imagine them wearing a T-shirt with the coded message that says, "Let me help. Give me choices."

3. **Revenge:** "I feel hurt when you treat me as though I am insignificant. I believe my only choice is to hurt you back."

   When teens feel hurt or believe that things are unfair, they often strike back with hurtful behavior. Then parents feel hurt and strike back, which hurts their teens. Thus, a revenge cycle is created. It is the adult's responsibility to understand what is happening and to break the cycle. The "Mistaken Goals" chart above can help you do this if you imagine your teen wearing a T-shirt with the coded message that says, "I'm hurting. Validate my feelings."

4. **Assumed inadequacy:** "I feel like giving up because I don't know what to do. I don't feel significant at all."

   It would be very rare to find a teen who truly is inadequate. However, teens can become so discouraged that they believe and act as though they are. They give up instead of trying. Telling teens that they are not inadequate does not help. Instead, parents need to find ways to help teens change their perceptions of inadequacy. Imagine this teen wearing a T-shirt with the coded message that says, "Don't give up on me. Show me a small step."

5. **Excitement seeking:** "I'm bored and looking for a rush."

   We don't include excitement seeking on the "Mistaken Goals" chart because it can fit in any of the four mistaken beliefs. It can be part of undue attention (Look at me. See how cool I am.); misguided power (No one can stop me. I'm invincible.); revenge

(I'll show you.); or assumed inadequacy (This is all I'm good for. It doesn't really matter.)

Excitement seeking leads teens to go after novelty, risk taking, and intense sensations. Discouraged teens seek excitement in negative ways, sometimes to show off (undue attention), sometimes for the power surge (misguided power), sometimes to get even for your lack of faith in them (revenge), and sometimes because they feel so hopeless that there's no point in trying anything else (assumed inadequacy). Many experiment with drugs, drive too fast, or have sex without regard to consequences. The challenge for parents is to encourage positive excitement seeking. Snowboarding, mountain climbing, playing sports, visiting foreign countries, volunteering after disasters, and taking challenging courses are positive solutions. Imagine this teen wearing a T-shirt with the coded message that says, "Help me find positive and safe excitement."

Understanding mistaken goals can help you see that whatever your teens do, they do because it makes sense to them. Just because you aren't aware of their logic doesn't mean it isn't there.

## IDENTIFYING A MISTAKEN GOAL

The easiest way to understand which mistaken goal your teen operates from is to tap into your own feelings. (See the second column of the "Mistaken Goals" chart.) If you're irritated, annoyed, feeling sorry for your child, worried, or exhausted from giving special attention or special service, the teen's goal is probably a need for undue attention. Feelings of anger, challenge, or defeat let you know the mistaken goal is misguided power. If you are hurt, disgusted, or disbelieving, the mistaken goal is probably revenge. If you feel a sense of despair and hopelessness and think nothing will ever change, your teen's mistaken goal is assumed inadequacy (your child assumes his or her skills are inadequate or nonexistent). If you feel panicked, fearful, or terrified, your teen is probably an excitement seeker.

Following are two examples of how caring adults used the "Mistaken Goals" chart to discover the mistaken beliefs of two teenagers and then, using encouragement, to change their beliefs and behavior.

### Assumed Inadequacy

Adam was feeling depressed and kept telling his parents how unhappy he was because he didn't have a girlfriend. He was the only kid in his circle of friends who hadn't invited someone to homecoming. No matter what his parents said to help cheer him up or empathize with him, Adam insisted that no matter what he did, no girl would ever go out with him. Adam's parents were so concerned about him that they suggested he talk to the family counselor. Even though they wanted to be good listeners, they thought they were over their heads. Sometimes there's a relative who can serve as a good listener, but often, a few trips to the counselor's office can end with much better communication between parent and teen.

When Adam came in to share his story, the counselor realized that Adam had a mistaken idea that no matter what he did, he would fail. Therefore he believed it was better not to try at all. Adam was convinced that girls didn't like him because he was shy. He believed that if he even attempted to talk to a girl, she would be bored and tell all her friends what a jerk he was. When the counselor asked where he got this idea, Adam mentioned that he had overheard some of the girls at school talking about a guy who had called them the night before. The girls laughed and shared stories of how they would get rid of this guy if he called any of them. Adam knew he didn't want to make a fool of himself like this guy.

When teens are that discouraged, the job of the parent or counselor is to help them get their courage back. The coded message is, "Don't give up on me. Show me a small step." By telling teens who have the mistaken goal of assumed inadequacy, "I have faith in you," "I won't give up on you," and "Here's a small step you could take if you like," adults help them work through the issue.

Adam's counselor asked him if he would be willing to look at the situation another way. Adam agreed. The counselor then asked Adam if he had ever purchased any clothing for himself. With a puzzled look he replied that he had just purchased a new ski jacket. "Did you just grab the first jacket you saw on the rack?" asked the counselor.

Adam said, "Of course not! I must have tried on about twenty to thirty jackets before I found the right one."

"Well, Adam," said the counselor, "do you think picking a girl to go to homecoming should be any easier?"

"I never thought of it that way," said Adam. "But what if I call someone and she tells her friends what a jerk I am?"

"You could tell yourself how grateful you are that a girl that rude decided not to go out with you."

Adam thought about all this and said, "It makes a lot of sense, but I still feel scared to talk to a girl. What if I can't think of anything to say?"

Adam and the counselor role-played calling girls, with different reactions to Adam's introduction. Adam realized that if a girl answered the phone with a little bit of enthusiasm, he would find it easier to think of things to talk about. If a girl was quiet and uncomfortable, Adam realized she might not be the right person for him to spend his first date with.

Adam was almost ready to go home and call someone, but he got cold feet one more time. The counselor noticed how scared he was and asked Adam if he had ever pushed through any fear in his life. Adam thought for a few minutes and then replied, "I used to be afraid to ski down really steep hills that had moguls on them, but now I love to."

"How did you manage to overcome your fear?"

"I stood at the top of the hill with my knees shaking and said to myself, 'Go for it!,' and I did. It was wonderful."

"Well, Adam," said the counselor. "Go for it!"

Adam grinned.

Adam was able to take steps toward correcting his perception of inadequacy because no one said to him, "It's silly to feel that way." Instead his parents listened well enough to know he needed help. His counselor listened, empathized, and explored the basis for his perception. She then helped him work on skills, based on his own experiences with success, to help him overcome his fears.

### Excitement Seeking

Tessa loved sneaking out of the house at night, climbing out of her window, and meeting up with friends. The group of girls would roam the streets for hours and their parents were none the wiser. The teens weren't looking for trouble, but one night, trouble found them. A group of guys spotted them and started harassing them. One of the guys pulled a knife and threatened to hurt someone if the girls didn't do what he wanted. The girls ran screaming in five different directions while the guys stood there laughing.

Tessa's mom noticed some comments on Tessa's Facebook, put two and two together, and realized what was going on. She asked Tessa to go for a walk with her so they could talk.

Mom started the conversation by saying, "Honey, I was a teen once myself, and I remember thinking I was invincible and that nothing bad could ever happen to me. I did some stupid things, which when I look back on them, I feel lucky to be alive. I want you to know I was scrolling through your Facebook as we've agreed I can do, and I saw the comments about last night. We need to talk about that."

Tessa interrupted saying, "Am I going to be grounded?"

"Is that what you want me to do?" Mom asked.

"No, it's not. I want you to trust me that I realized my friends and I made a big mistake roaming the streets so late at night. It was a lot of fun for a long time, but after what happened last night, I don't want to do that again. I thought that guy with the knife was going to kill one of us. That wasn't fun."

"Oh, honey, I'm sorry you were so scared, but I am glad that you are deciding not to roam around like that. If you're needing more excitement in your life, maybe we can think of some alternatives."

"Mom, last night was all the excitement I'll need for a long time. If I get bored and need help figuring out what to do for thrills, I promise to talk to you first."

"Okay, but just in case you might want another suggestion, can I give you one?"

"Mom, what?"

"I just read about a bunch of full-moon hikes and kayaking adventures in our area. If you and your friends are interested, I'm willing to sign you up, pay for the registration, and drive you guys to the event. Why don't you talk to your friends and see what they think."

"Hey, that might be fun. If we do it, though, I'm pretty sure we'd want to drive ourselves there. We're not kids anymore, Mom."

"Point taken. Keep me posted."

Awareness of mistaken goals is the first step toward change. It takes two to fuel mistaken-goal behavior. If your teen seeks undue attention, it could be that you have not taken enough time for training in how to get attention in useful ways. We have never seen a power-drunk teen without a power-drunk adult close by. Involving teens in problem solving is one way to help them use their power usefully. They need many of these opportunities. If your teen hurts you, then he or she probably feels hurt by you. Another possibility is that your teens may feel hurt by others and take their feelings out on you. If your teen is giving up, it could be that he thinks he can't live up to expectations. Clues for encouraging discouraged teens are in the last column of the "Mistaken Goals" chart.

Remember that the perceptions teens have and the decisions they make about their experiences color their pictures of themselves and help explain some of their behavior. It's also helpful to remember that your teen's reality may be different from your own.

Once you understand the mistaken goal, you'll find there are many ways to encourage your teen and improve a situation. Then you can actively attempt to make things better, rather than merely reacting to your child's behavior.

## FOUR PERSONALITY TYPES INCREASE UNDERSTANDING

The four personality types, each with different needs and behaviors, provide another way to help you understand yourself and your teen. It's possible that the things that annoy you about your teen (and vice versa) may be characteristics of his or her personality type and not intentional behaviors meant to upset each other. We call these personalities "Top Cards." You can learn more about Top Card in many of our books, including *Positive Discipline* by Jane Nelsen and *Do It Yourself Therapy* by Lynn Lott, Riki Intner, and Barbara Mendenhall.

Start by answering the following question: What would you most want to avoid dealing with—pain and stress, rejection and hassles, meaninglessness and unimportance, or criticism and ridicule? You can only pick one group of words and if the words don't make sense to you, they aren't the words you need to worry about. Each top card is represented by an animal. If you picked pain and stress, you're a turtle and your top card is called Comfort/Avoidance. Rejection and hassles? You're a chameleon and your top card is called Pleasing. Meaninglessness and unimportance means you're a lion and your top card is called Superiority. And criticism and ridicule makes you an eagle with a top card called Control.

Look at the chart on pages 202–205 to learn more about yourself and your teen. Then think of things you may be doing that simply don't work with a different animal.

If your teen is a chameleon and feeling stressed and you're a lion parent, think of the difficulties if you are digging in and getting stubborn and fighting with her when all she is looking for is approval and appreciation. Or what if you are a stressed turtle parent micromanaging and spoiling an eagle teen who wants to do things himself when he's stressed and puts up a wall the more you try to help. You can use the chart in many ways to find out what works and what doesn't work for the various combinations of parents and teens.

## YOU DON'T HAVE TO DO THIS ALONE

Even though this is a book for parents of teens, and even though the suggestions and information are geared toward what parents can learn and do to improve relationships, we don't want to give the idea that it's all up to the parents to make changes. Teens who read this book give us very positive feedback and agree with much of what we say. They highly recommend the book to their parents. But they also get some ideas about things they can do differently to make relationships better. We encourage you to get your teens involved, inviting them to do the activities with you. Suggest to your teens that they might find helpful hints to help you improve your parenting and that they might also learn some things that would be fun to share with their friends.

When you understand that your teen's behavior is more a result of unconscious perceptions than of anything else, you'll stop looking for causes and diseases and start looking for your teen's separate reality. With this understanding as your foundation, you'll find it easier to focus on the many skills you have learned for encouraging your teen—and yourself in the process.

### KIND AND FIRM PARENTING TOOLS TO REMEMBER

1. Your teens have opinions about themselves based on their place in the family pie. Reviewing the information about birth order can be extremely helpful to you for understanding your teens better.
2. All behavior has a purpose, even if your child (and you) aren't aware of what the purpose is. When you notice your feelings, you get valuable information about what the purpose of your teen's behavior might be.
3. Instead of reacting to behavior, use the "Mistaken Goals" chart for inspiration.
4. Once you know which animal you are, it is easier to realize that the "care and feeding" of each creature is different.

## TOP CARD

| If You Chose | Then Your Personality Style Is Called | And Perhaps When You Are Stressed You Do the Following | When You Aren't Stressed, You Have Many Assets and Gifts | Here Are Some of the Problems You Invite or Struggle With | What You Need from Others When You Are Stressed Is | What You Need to Work on Is | What You Long for Is |
|---|---|---|---|---|---|---|---|
| Rejection and Hassles | Pleasing (You're like the Chameleon) | Act friendly. Say yes and mean no. Give in. Worry about what others want more than your needs. Gossip instead of confronting directly. Try to fix everything and make everybody happy. Beg for understanding. Complain when not appreciated. Accommodate. Work hard. Catastrophize. Get silent, like a deer in the headlights. Be super reasonable and avoid your feelings. Whine or feel sorry for yourself. | Sensitive to others. Have lots of friends. Considerate. Compromiser. Non-threatening. Likely to volunteer. People count on you. Usually see positives in people and things. Can be a loving and loveable person when you aren't seeking approval. | Invite revenge cycles and others to feel rejected when they don't appreciate all you do for "them." Feel resentful and ignored when people don't read your mind to give you what you want. Get in trouble for trying to look good while doing bad. (At least I feel guilty, so that must make me a good person.) Loss of sense of self and what pleases you. (Want others to read your mind and to please you.) | Tell you how much they love you. Touch you a lot. Show approval. Show appreciation. Let you know you won't be in trouble if you say how you really feel. | Be more open and honest and say what you are thinking and feeling. Say no and mean it. Let others have their feelings and let their behavior be about them and not you. Spend time alone and give up trying to please everyone. Ask others what would please them instead of you getting to decide. Don't be afraid to ask for help or for another perspective. | To do what you want while others clap. For others to like you, accept you and be flexible. For others to take care of you and make hassles go away. |

| If You Chose | Then Your Personality Style Is Called | And Perhaps When You Are Stressed You Do the Following | When You Aren't Stressed, You Have Many Assets and Gifts | Here Are Some of the Problems You Invite or Struggle With | What You Need from Others When You Are Stressed Is | What You Need to Work On Is | What You Long for Is |
|---|---|---|---|---|---|---|---|
| Criticism and Ridicule | Control (You're like the Eagle) | Hold back. Boss others. Organize. Argue. Get quiet and wait for others to coax you. Do it yourself. Stuff your feelings. Cover all the bases before you make a move. Complain, sigh, get angry. Procrastinate. Explain/defend. Engage in physical activity. Put up a wall. | Good leader and crisis manager. Assertive. Persistent. Well organized. Productive. Law abiding. Get what you want. Able to get things done and figure things out. Take charge of situations. Wait patiently. Can be a person of generosity and equanimity when you aren't seeking control. | Lack spontaneity. Social and emotional distance. Want to keep others from finding weak spots. Invite power struggles. Avoid dealing with issues when you feel criticized. Get defensive instead of being open. Sometimes wait for permission. Critical and fault finding even though you don't like being on the receiving end. | Say OK. Give you choices. Let you lead. Ask how you feel. Give you time and space to sort out your feelings. | Remind yourself that you are not responsible for another. Stop trying to prevent problems you don't have and take a small action step. Stop and listen to others instead of withdrawing. Think about what you want and ask for it. Listen instead of getting defensive. Ask for help and choices. Delegate. Be curious. | To be in control even though others can be better, smarter. To get respect, cooperation and loyalty. For others to have faith in you and give you permission to do what you want. To have choices and go at your own pace. |

| If You Chose | Then Your Personality Style Is Called | And Perhaps When You Are Stressed You Do the Following | When You Aren't Stressed, You Have Many Assets and Gifts | Here Are Some of the Problems You Invite or Struggle With | What You Need from Others When You Are Stressed Is | What You Need to Work On Is | What You Long for Is |
|---|---|---|---|---|---|---|---|
| Meaninglessness and Unimportance | Superiority (You're like the Lion) | Put down people or things. Knock yourself. Talk about the absurdity of life. Correct others. Overdo. Take on too much. Worry about always doing better. Operate on shoulds. Cry, scream, or complain to others. Dig in and get stubborn. Be indecisive. Become the expert. Seek advocates. Fight whether or not it is necessary. | Knowledgeable. Precise. Idealistic. Get a lot done. Make people laugh. Receive a lot of praise, awards, and prizes. Don't have to wait for others to tell you what to do to get things done. Have a lot of self-confidence. Can be a person of depth and significance when you aren't seeking status. Inspire others. | Overwhelmed, overburdened. Invite others to feel incapable and insignificant. Seen as a know-it-all or rude and insulting and don't know it's a problem. Never happy because you could have done more or better. Have to put up with so many imperfect people around you. Sometimes you don't do anything. Spend too much time doubting your worth. | Tell you how significant you are. Thank you for your contributions. Help you get started with a small step. Tell you you're right. Tell you you're special and important. | Stop looking for blame and start working on solutions. Give credit where credit is due, including to yourself. Look at what you have instead of what you don't have. Show an interest in others and be curious about them. Go for a walk, exercise, eat something healthy. | To prove your worth by being the best. To get appreciation and recognition from others. Spiritual connection. To be recognized for being right and for making a difference. |

| If You Chose | Then Your Personality Style Is Called | And Perhaps When You Are Stressed You Do the Following | When You Aren't Stressed, You Have Many Assets and Gifts | Here Are Some of the Problems You Invite or Struggle With | What You Need from Others When You Are Stressed Is | What You Need to Work On Is | What You Long for Is |
|---|---|---|---|---|---|---|---|
| Pain and Stress | Comfort or avoidance (You're like the Turtle) | Make jokes. Intellectualize. Do only the things you already do well. Avoid new experiences. Take the path of least resistance. Leave sentences incomplete. Avoid risks. Hide so no one can find you aren't perfect. Overreact. Complain. Cry. Scream. Micromanage and spoil others. Don't ask for help. Tuck back into your shell. Attack like a snapping turtle. Close up your heart. | People enjoy being around you. Flexible. Highly creative. Do what you do well. Easygoing. Look out for self and own needs. Can count on others to help. Make others feel comfortable. Can be a person of courage and grace when you aren't seeking comfort. | Suffer boredom. Lazy, lack of productivity. Hard to motivate. Don't do your share. Invite special attention and service. Worry a lot but no one knows how scared you are. Lose out on the contact of sharing. Juggle uncomfortable situations rather than confront them. Wait to be taken care of instead of becoming independent. Invites others to feel annoyed and bored. | Not interrupting. Invite your comments. Listen quietly. Leave room for you. Show faith. Encourage small steps. | Create a routine for yourself. Show up and stick around, even if all you do at first is watch. Speak up and ask questions or say what you want instead of assuming. Tell others how you are feeling. Ask someone to do things with you at your pace till you feel comfortable. Share your talents with others. | For things to be as easy as they look. To be left alone, to have your own space and pace. You don't want to argue. |

*Practical Application Activity*

### Breaking the Mistaken Goal Cycle
Find out how you might be part of the problem.

1. Talk with an objective friend or therapist.
2. Write in a journal. You often gain insight when you review in writing what actually has happened between you and your teen.
3. Ask your teen. Let your teenager know you are not a mind reader. Admit that you might not have been a good listener in the past, but you want to listen now. You may suggest that you contributed to the problem. (Even little kids, when told, "I think I did something to hurt your feelings," can tell you what you did.)
4. Look at the "Mistaken Goals" chart for ideas and inspiration.

Make some guesses out loud to your teen about what you are thinking might be going on. If your guess is correct, you'll hit a responsive chord; your child will feel understood and will acknowledge the accurateness of the guess. On the other hand, it's okay if your guess is incorrect. Your aim is not to be right but to get information. If you're wrong, you've still learned something.

When you understand your teen's perception, validate him or her. Let your child know that you can see how he or she might have come to that conclusion. Then, plan together to make changes that are supportive of both of you.

# 13

# WHAT DO YOU DO ABOUT SCARY BEHAVIOR?

## DEVELOPING FAITH IN YOURSELF AND YOUR TEEN

Certain scary topics come up time and again in our parenting classes and workshops. Those subjects are the focus of this chapter. The topics include friends; gangs and bullies; drugs and other addictive behaviors; sexual activity and AIDS; sexual abuse; cutting, suicidal behaviors; eating problems; and young adults who won't or can't leave home. Let's start with the least scary, but one that's scary nonetheless.

## FRIENDS, OR LACK THEREOF

Having a teen who can't seem to get along with peers or who isolates him- or herself beyond what seems like a reasonable amount of time can be scary. If your teen is willing to hear some tips, we recommend the following:

- Be aware of the energy you create with your thoughts and feelings about yourself. If you feel insecure, you'll act insecure. If you feel confident, you will act confident. Confidence energy is attractive. Insecurity energy is not. We are not suggesting you act like a phony and project something you don't feel. Awareness is the first step. If you aren't feeling confident, see if you can figure out ways to increase your confidence.

- Don't do to others what you don't want them to do to you. Instead of gossiping behind someone's back, talk to that person directly. Don't start or spread rumors.

- Practice smiling when you walk through the halls at school. Again, this does not mean a phony smile. Think of something that makes you feel happy, and the smile will follow.

- Be curious about others. Ask other kids questions about themselves based on real interest.

You might want to encourage opportunities for your teen to get involved in activities in which he or she can meet teenagers with similar interests. Joining a ski club or a gym or getting involved in drama, dance, karate, chess club, or a youth group at church are great ways to meet folks with common interests. Sometimes you have to take a heavy hand and insist that your teen must try something four times before quitting. We are often impressed at the number of young people who need just this kind of help from their parents.

You can also help your teens explore, through a friendly conversation, what they think the long-term results of their behaviors might be. If they are critical of everyone or afraid to ask to join in and instead wait at home to be called, they might have few friends. Your teens might find the following story both humorous and inspiring.

Dr. Lew Losoncy, once a shy teenager, is now a motivational speaker and author of more than sixteen books, including *Salon Psychology:*

*How to Succeed with People and Be a Positive Person.* During a lecture at a NASAP (North American Society of Adlerian Psychology) conference, Lew shared a story about how embarrassed he felt while walking down the street with his friend who would ask just about every girl he saw for a date. His friend was rejected 80 percent of the time. However, every Saturday night, while Lew spent the evening at home, his friend was out on a date. After all, 20 percent said, "Yes." We aren't suggesting that your teens ask every girl or boy they meet for a date, but they might want to take a few risks that might invite rejection—and might not.

You could also watch your own behavior. If you tell your teens how to behave, you'll probably have very little influence. But, remember, your teens do watch how you act, and they often mimic your worst habits. For example, do you yell at people on the freeway or talk about a person's "stupid" behavior? Do you talk down to salespeople or service providers? Don't be surprised if your negative child has taken a page out of your book.

Sometimes the best approach for helping a teen with peer relations is to butt out and let him or her work it through. This is an especially good idea when teens make a situation much worse than it really is. Your teens may turn a fight with a friend into a belief that they don't have a friend in the entire world. Usually after a day or two, all is well again. However, if you butt into this situation, it may get dragged out and made worse than it really is.

## WHEN YOU DISLIKE YOUR TEENS' FRIENDS

Many battles are fought when teens choose friends their parents do not approve of. This is a reasonable concern for many parents, because friends do have an influence on each other's choices and behaviors. However, the way most parents handle this problem only intensifies the battle, driving teens to be even more loyal to each other. We know of very few (actually none, but we imagine there must be some) parents who have been successful at forbidding their teens to have certain friends. Because parents can't monitor every moment of their teens' days, it is impossible to control who your teens have as friends.

Instead of controlling your teen's friends, try the opposite. Welcome them into your home. Be friendly and joke around with them. You have more influence when you create a welcoming home environment where your teen feels more comfortable. When you give your teens this kind of space, they often tire of the friend on their own. Also, the bad behavior of some teens could be an indication that this friend does not have an encouraging home environment. Hanging out in your home could be the opportunity for him or her to experience encouragement.

If you are worried about the influence that other teens have on your own, be honest about your fears. Use some of the methods discussed in this book—role-play, family meetings, joint problem solving, and curiosity questions—so your teen will be equipped with more skills for dealing with potentially dangerous situations. Doing so not only provides opportunities for you to discuss your feelings, but also provides your teen with skills to think and prepare ahead. Of course, this doesn't guarantee that mistakes won't be made, but it does decrease the chances.

Keep in mind that just as your teens' behaviors aren't forever, their friends' behaviors aren't forever either. Many parents, after learning what fine people some of their teens' friends have turned out to be, have been embarrassed that they had treated them so poorly.

## BULLIES

Now to some of the scarier problems teens and their parents face. Young people must be taken very seriously when they ask for your help or the school's help to deal with prejudice, violence, sexting, cyberbullying, or other safety issues. If they don't ask for help, it is up to adults to be vigilant about bullying and aggressive behaviors and to intervene in the problem. The most effective solutions for bullying are those that involve the entire community whether it is the family or the school. Class meetings, circle meetings, restorative justice programs, and family meetings are all appropriate places to talk about what is going on and to create solutions and clarify consequences.

There are many programs that teach victims to make friends with bullies to stop the bullying. We recommend that all players in the bullying cycle get help with encouragement and empowerment: bullies can learn empathy and appropriate places to deal with a need for attention, power, and justice; victims can learn to stop feeding into the bully's behavior and be less isolated; and observers can learn to intervene as peacemakers or help create safe spaces for all in their schools. All these skills can be learned in the class meeting.

Bullying behavior can be physical, verbal, or emotional and happens when someone with more power or social support picks on someone with less. It can happen in person or over the Internet. Any solution needs to include the bully, the victim, and the bystanders as all are affected and involved in the problem. Many schools have programs to help with bullying. Expecting kids to deal with this alone is unrealistic. In the most extreme situations, kids who've been bullied excessively have either killed themselves or taken a gun to school and shot classmates and teachers.

Most people focus on the wrong solutions for violence in schools. They talk about gun control, uniforms, corporal punishment, guards, identifying and punishing the bullies, and holding parents accountable. What very few discuss is the value of teaching kids self-discipline, responsibility, respect for self and others, and problem-solving skills—all of which teens learn when they participate in regular and effective class meetings. (See *Positive Discipline in the Classroom,* Revised 3rd Edition, by Jane Nelsen, Lynn Lott, and H. Stephen Glenn, Three Rivers Press.) Schools tend to encounter fewer problems when they use class meetings (including compliments and problem solving) to help every student feel a sense of belonging and to teach students how to use their power in constructive ways. It is difficult to dismiss the importance of compliments in class meetings when you read the statement Eric Harris (Columbine killer) wrote in his diary (quoted in *Newsweek*, July 17, 2006): "If people would give me more compliments, all of this might still be avoidable."

As your children get older, they may end up being confronted by a bully who threatens, intimidates, or steals from them. That's what happened to Geoff, who woke up every day afraid to go to school. He was picked on over and over, probably because he was shy and dressed differently from the other kids. At first a group of boys taunted him with words, but soon the bullying escalated to shoving and tripping. It didn't take long before the group of boys who were bullying Geoff started posting rumors on a social network site that Geoff was gay, something they made up.

Geoff's schoolwork started to suffer, and he began having stomach pains. He was afraid to use the bathroom at school for fear that he'd get harassed or that one of the kids would try to give him a wedgie (pulling his underwear up from behind until it hurt). It never occurred to Geoff that the guy who was the ringleader of the group that made his life unbearable was suffering from his own insecurities, trying to look like a big shot with his peers.

Without adult intervention, Geoff's situation wasn't going to get better. Geoff was too embarrassed to talk to anyone about what was going on, and he was afraid if he told on the bullies, their behavior would get worse. Fortunately for Geoff, his parents noticed his decline and told him they were scheduling a meeting with the school counselor. With some prodding, the bullying story came out and the counselor said he would look into the situation without mentioning Geoff's name. He also suggested that Geoff ignore the bully and walk away, that he could practice confidence even if he had to fake it, and that he should think about joining a class, an after-school group, or a club where he could make some friends. Most important, the counselor encouraged Geoff to talk about what was going on with either him or his parents so that he didn't have to be alone and could get adult support for his feelings. What helped the most was when Geoff made a friend who said, "I saw that stuff people wrote about you on MySpace and I didn't believe a word of it. Want to come over to my place and play some video games?"

The best defense to teach your teens is a good offense. Teach or give permission for your son or daughter to let a bully know, in no uncertain terms, to leave their stuff alone. Using the same voice he or she uses when a sibling invades his or her space is most effective. You may also choose to send your teen to self-defense classes, which greatly changes the way your child thinks of and carries him- or herself. You're not training your teens to become lethal weapons or to meet violence with violence; rather, you are providing your teens with self-confidence and the ability to defend themselves, which usually makes the actual defending unnecessary.

## DRUG USE AND OTHER ADDICTIVE BEHAVIORS

The fear of drug abuse is the number one problem plaguing parents of teens today. You've heard the stories of teenage deaths and ruined lives from drug overdoses or drug- and alcohol-related accidents. You've heard of parties where kids empty all the pills from their parents' medicine cabinet into a container and then grab handfuls that they wash down to see what happens. You know that someone could slip something into a drink at a party and your teen could take a "trip" she never intended, possibly ending in rape or worse. Just like most other parents, you are probably struggling with what to do about all this information.

Many parents fear drug abuse because they used or abused drugs themselves when they were younger. Many of these parents worry that their teens will do what they did but won't recover. Other parents never used drugs but have many fears and judgments about drug use. Some parents don't even realize that drugs are a potential problem until they find out their teen is using. These parents usually stumble on the information by discovering drug paraphernalia by accident, or a car filled with empty beer cans or liquor bottles.

There are other signs of drug abuse, such as dramatic changes in behavior, aggressiveness, depression, alteration in sleep or eating habits, weight loss, spaciness, and lack of concern for activities that used to be important. Some well-meaning professionals misinterpret these behaviors as mental illness. We feel sad that many parents prefer having their child diagnosed with a mental illness rather than admitting their son or daughter has a drug problem or is an addict.

There's a lot of denial about drug use and abuse, which we think of as misinformation and misunderstanding. We've come across professionals who have said that marijuana isn't addictive and is probably even good for your teen. They are sure no one has ever gone through withdrawal giving up marijuana. This is false information given the amount of anxiety, paranoia, and inability to function many people go through when they stop regular use.

Other misinformation includes overlooking certain substances, such as tobacco, alcohol, and prescription or over-the-counter drugs, and not realizing they are addictive drugs. Then there are the substances that you may not know about, such as GHB and "roofies," not to mention the ones you probably do know about, including cocaine, inhalants, ecstasy, heroin, amphetamines, barbiturates, and hallucinogens.

If drugs are so scary to parents and potentially damaging to teens, why are they so popular? Some teens say they want to experiment and find out what effect the substance has; others say they like to be part of the group; still others say they think using substances makes them less shy, less boring, freer, faster, sexier, more fun, more relaxed, and happier. Many teens use drugs to emulate their idols in the entertainment world or famous writers who have glorified drug use. Some enjoy the escape to a different reality or "feeling place." Young people will use speed to lose weight or stay awake to study for finals, or a date may give a sedative to a girl to make her *out of it* and forgetful so he can force sex on her without getting caught. Some teens use drugs because they think it makes them more grown-up. Others say someone they thought was cool introduced them to drugs, and they wanted to be just like that person, so they started using.

In spite of the side effects of damaged relationships with parents and old friends, hangovers, nausea, vomiting, blackouts, mood swings, rapid heartbeats, reduced inhibitions, breathing difficulties, or even the possibility of death, teens continue to use substances until they decide not to.

Teens have grown up in a culture that stresses the "short-term feel good" and the "quick fix." Therefore, using drugs fits in with the cultural norm. Many teens lack a feeling-words vocabulary. They don't have a person with whom they feel safe talking or a place where it is safe to express feelings. For these teens, drugs provide a way to numb feelings and make problems seem to disappear. Overcontrolled or overprotected young people will use drugs as a way to rebel against parental controls.

### Parental Fear Is a Natural Response to Information About Teen Drug Use

No wonder you are frightened. Maybe you're remembering some of your own drug experiences or recalling a friend or family member who has struggled with addiction. Much of the current literature suggests that you should know what is going on in your teens' lives at all times. These books tell you to monitor your teens' friendships, supervise their relationships, communicate with other parents, supervise teen parties, and refuse to let teens go anywhere that they might encounter drugs.

The question often comes up, "Should you search your kid's room?" If you feel a need to do that, rather than sneaking around, knock on your teen's door, let your child know you are worried about his or her behavior and that you are afraid your teen is hiding things from you that may affect his or her safety. Let your teens know you would like them to talk honestly with you without getting in trouble. If your teens refuse to talk to you, make it clear that you will be searching their rooms without their permission and that you will be calling for professional help. Make it clear that you love your teens too much to risk having them hurt others or themselves and that the situation has gotten too far out of control to ignore it or hope it will fix itself.

You are told that these methods (searching rooms, knowing every detail of your child's life at all times, monitoring friendships, supervising relationships, communicating with other parents, supervising teen parties, and refusing to let teens go anywhere they might encounter drugs) will protect your kids from using or abusing drugs. This is an overly simplistic and unrealistic statement when you consider what is really going on and how ineffective those methods really are.

We have talked with hundreds of teenagers—really good kids—and it is so sad to hear how they feel they have to walk on eggshells around their parents. They would love to talk with them and have a nonjudgmental conversation to explore their experiences and figure out what they mean, but they are afraid of the disapproval, the disappointment, or of getting into trouble. So what do they do instead? They sneak around, they lie, they avoid, and they rebel. They feel sad, hurt, anxious, and angry.

When parents wonder why their children lie, we tell them, "Because they love you. They need to individuate (find out who they are separate from you), and they don't want to disappoint you. So they explore and test and break the rules; and then they lie so they don't have to experience your disappointment or your wrath."

Not all children feel they have to lie. Some can talk to their parents. Two teenagers shared their envy of a friend who could tell his parents everything. Their friend even told his parents that he had tried drinking at a party. Instead of going ballistic, these parents helped him explore his experience. They asked curiosity questions, starting with asking him how he felt about it—*and then they listened*. They asked him how he felt about responsible drinking and irresponsible drinking, and if he knew the difference. *And then they listened.*

They were not surprised at how much their son had thought about his life because they had always taught him to think for himself and to *explore* the consequences of his choices with their supportive help (very different from *imposing* consequences). It was obvious that their son had thought a lot about drinking. He told them he really didn't want to get drunk and act silly like the other kids did. He knew that he didn't want drinking to be a daily habit for him, and certainly didn't want to be an alcoholic. He said he would never drink and drive, and he had even taken keys away from a friend who was drunk and wanted to drive. (Very responsible.)

They wondered if he ever drank when he didn't want to because of peer pressure. He admitted that he had. They avoided any lectures about that and just let him sit with that information. Several weeks later he told his parents he had decided not to drink when he didn't feel like it and didn't feel any peer pressure. Instead his friends said, "Cool. You can be our designated driver."

Another teenager said, "I wish I could talk to my parents about everything, but I can talk to them only about the things that are safe, such as sports. My parents know I'm good at sports, but they don't really know anything about the issues I struggle with. They know who they think I am, or who they want me to be, but they don't know who I really am."

### Suggestions for Dealing with Teens and Drugs

Given all this information about drug use, you're still probably asking, "What can I do?" Some teens won't use drugs if you tell them you don't want them to, so go ahead and say it if it's how you feel.

You may choose to show your concern about drug problems by getting involved with drug-free dances, safe parties, safe-ride programs, and the just-say-no program. Even though it's unrealistic to think that these activities by themselves can tackle the drug problem, all efforts are important—and these programs have made a difference. If anything, you will probably feel better knowing you are doing something, anything, to make a difference.

Even if you think your teens won't drink, make sure they understand the effect of alcohol on their systems. It is tragic to hear of teens who have died because they drank too much, fell asleep, and choked on their vomit. These tragedies may have been averted if some adult had told them that just because vodka mixed with fruit juice goes down easily, their blood alcohol level is such that they can poison their system even if they don't feel the effect at the moment. When that happens, people lose consciousness and can die.

Caution your kids that if they see any of these signs in a friend, they need to get help immediately: mental confusion or the person has passed out and can't be awoken; vomiting; seizures; slow breathing (fewer than eight breaths per minute); irregular breathing (ten seconds or more between breaths); hypothermia (low body temperature), bluish skin color, and/or paleness (see www.hazelden.org/web/public/ade90201.page). The Hazelden article further recommends that after calling 911, gently turn this person on his or her side to prevent choking after vomiting.

The best way to help your kids make intelligent decisions about drugs is to empower them in all the ways we've been suggesting in this book. When your teens have opportunities to contribute, when they feel listened to and taken seriously and know they can talk to you about what is really going on, and when you provide opportunities for them to learn skills and experience success, they are less likely to abuse drugs. Notice we say abuse drugs, not use drugs. Your teens may choose to use drugs whether you like it or not, whether you remain vigilant or not. This is reality. Teens who have the self-confidence and skills we have been discussing are likely to experiment with alcohol and drugs, but they are less likely to abuse them.

### The Continuum of Use

There are different kinds of drug use. People without information think of drug abuse as the only alternative to abstinence. The continuum of drug use moves from abstinence (no use) at one end to chemical dependency at the other, with experimentation, social use, regular use, and problem use in between. Being aware that there are differences can be helpful to you, and your response to the problem needs to match the type of use. It's also helpful to talk about the continuum of use with your kids. There is no indication that if someone starts at one end of the continuum, they will automatically continue to the other end.

**Experimental use** means "I heard about it. I want to try it out. I want to know what it feels like. A bunch of us are going to get together and find out what happens when we get drunk, or what happens when we take pills." A teen experimenting may try a drug once and never again.

This may not make drug use any less scary for you, but we suggest you don't overreact. Encourage a friendly discussion and share your fears that your teen may be getting into something that could become dangerous, and you wish he or she would stop now. Some of you may be reassured to know that teens who party have often seen what happens when someone has a "bad trip"; these kids have their own limits and methods for trying out only what they feel safe doing. Many kids never go past the experimental phase of drug use.

**Social use** involves using drugs for social occasions without letting the drug take control. A social user can stop after a small amount of a drug, whereas an addict can't do just a little or stop. You may still be concerned, because whatever people practice, they get better at, and there are plenty of addicts out there who started using socially and ended up with a full-blown addiction. Say what you think, how you feel, and what you want, and make sure you are clear with your child. Then ask your teen what he or she thinks, feels, and wants. Be sure to listen. Be aware that many social users these days drink to get drunk and can see no reason to drink if that isn't going to happen. Using curiosity questions, explore with your teens the possible consequences of that type of drinking.

**Regular use** is drug use that has become ritualized and is thus potentially more dangerous because it could turn into an addiction. We have worked with many teens who get stoned every day or drink regularly and still are able to maintain their relationships, schoolwork, and their self-respect and dignity. However, many have moved into the next point on the continuum—problem use.

**Problem use** happens when teens' drug use leads to them having problems with managing their lives. They have problems with school, family, and work.

With teens especially, the more they use, the less they develop their skills to meet challenges and become competent. They use chemicals to repress their feelings instead of expressing them. They may even cause serious physical damage to themselves from prolonged use. If you think your teen's use is problematic, tell your child you love him and say that you want to help or get help with the problem. Don't accept promises for change. Although your teen may be sincere, he or she may not realize the hold the chemical has on the body. Also, when you talk with a person who has become addicted, you are not talking with a rational person. Don't expect reason. It won't happen. However, if you do get help at the problem use stage, you may be able to avoid the next stage. The line between problem use and chemical dependency is different for every person. Some people will never cross the line, others will. Some people become chemically dependent without going through all phases of the continuum.

**Chemical dependency** occurs when the drug is running your teen's life. Something that may start as an innocent activity can end up as a monster that takes over. In talking to several pot smokers who started around fourteen years old and kept up that habit well into their twenties and thirties, here are some of their comments:

> I have poisoned my body.
> I want to think clearly.
> Life is passing me by.
> I wish I could love myself.
> After a while, pot smoking isn't that much fun, but I can't
>    stop.
> It's the only thing I can enjoy.
> It's better than doing nothing.
> It makes boredom more interesting.
> It's a way to kill time.
> It's a full-time occupation.
> When I stopped smoking, I went through an extremely
>    difficult physical and emotional withdrawal. I thought I
>    was going crazy.

Many, if not most, of these people started smoking pot in their teens. When they started, they believed that pot was an herb, so they couldn't become addicted. Yet fifteen or more years later, they are still smoking dope as their primary activity and have failed numerous times to quit. Their lives revolve around growing or obtaining pot, smoking it, being stoned, getting stoned, or zoning out on pot. They are addicted and the drug is running their lives.

When you and your teens understand the continuum of drug use, you are both in a better place to evaluate what is going on and what to do about it. There are still too many stereotypes about what makes a real addict. One of the most prevalent myths is that there are gateway drugs (nicotine and pot seem to be the most popular), and once your child uses them, they open the door to all other drugs. Research tells us this is not true, and that drugs have different effects. Many young people like the effects of an upper but not a downer, or they prefer slowing down to revving up, or they like a drug that takes them out of their reality like a hallucinogen or opiate.

If you and your teen think addicts look like the folks you see sleeping in doorways, you could be minimizing the seriousness of your teen's relationship with drugs. The comments on page 220 so aptly describe the hopelessness and helplessness of addiction. If you met the contributors on the street, you'd never know they were addicts; if you read the comments, you can't help but hear the cries for help. They want help because the drugs have taken control away from them. If your teens are in this place, do whatever it takes to get them into treatment.

Whether you believe that drug abuse is a disease or a "solution," every problem user and addict knows that the behaviors stop when the user decides it will stop—and not before. Your job as a parent is to help your child make that decision, if you can. Usually, professional help is needed. Chemical dependency is like being on an elevator going down. People don't need to hit bottom before getting off—they can get off on any floor. With very few exceptions, however, once a person is chemically dependent, the only choice for breaking the cycle is abstinence along with interventions and with help (treatment, therapy, group help like Alcoholics Anonymous).

### Choosing a Therapist

If you need professional help, the most important criterion to consider in choosing a therapist is finding one your teen can relate to. Even though it is important for you to feel comfortable, you need to keep shopping until your teen is comfortable. Stay away from therapists who recommend a punitive, restrictive approach for parenting teens. It will just make things worse. We also recommend being very careful about a therapist who recommends prescription drugs. This is similar to putting duct tape over a gas gauge. Is it really helping to mask the problem with drugs instead of finding a good therapist who will help you deal with the problem?

If possible, ask people you know to refer a therapist with whom they have felt satisfied. If no one you know has been to a therapist, ask Al-Anon groups or church groups for referrals. When you find a therapist, don't hesitate to ask for a get-acquainted interview, so you can learn about his or her basic philosophy and you can tell the therapist about your perspectives on your teen.

Remember, when teenagers are chemically dependent, they will not want to see a therapist because they will want to protect their drug use. Find an Al-Anon group for yourself and work toward intervention.

### Interventions Can Happen at Any Time

Another way you can help your teen with drug problems is to use an intervention. Interventions are also on a continuum from informal to formal, with formal interventions occurring with the help of a trained interventionist. An intervention is a way for you to get out of denial and start dealing with what is really happening. Doing an intervention means you stop rescuing, overprotecting, controlling, or in any way taking responsibility for your teen's life. Instead, treat your teen as an adult-in-training and start saying only what you mean and following through with actions. Interventions require you to be gut-level honest and to stop playing games.

Some informal interventions happen when you begin to look at some of the messages you've inadvertently been giving your teen about drugs.

Do you use over-the-counter or prescription drugs to deal with all your feelings? Do you suggest a pill to make the pain go away whenever your teen is complaining? Do you zone out at the computer or in front of the TV, shop, read, or eat to avoid dealing with your feelings? If you answer yes to these questions, don't be afraid to open a dialogue with your teen about your awareness.

There is a wonderful intervention story about Gandhi. A mother came to him and said, "Please tell my child to stop eating sugar." Gandhi said, "Would you come back in three days?" The mother came back in three days with her child, and Gandhi said to the child, "Stop eating sugar." The mother asked, "Why did you have to wait three days to tell him that?" Gandhi said, "Well, I had to stop myself before I could tell him to stop."

### More Informal Interventions

Addison told his teenage son, "I'm concerned about your drinking. I notice that you drink a lot and drink fast. Your grandfather is an alcoholic, and research has shown that kids who have one or more relatives who are chemically dependent have an increased risk of becoming chemically dependent themselves. I hope you'll think about what I'm saying. I love you, and I wouldn't want you to go through the pain of addiction."

Clara told her teenagers, "I know there will be times you may decide to use drugs even though you know I'm against it. It's not okay with me to have drugs in our house or at any parties here. I realize that may create some problems for you, but I'm happy to help in any way to plan parties with you that can be fun without drugs. If you do decide to use drugs, I want you to know that even though I prefer that you don't, I love you and I'm here to listen and not judge you if you'd like my help or want to talk to me about it."

Bob told his twin boys, who insisted that pot wasn't a problem and that he was just uptight and didn't understand, "I'm not into this. You're right, I don't know much about it, but I really don't like it. I don't even approve of using pot. But I want to know what it's like for you. I want you to tell me more about it. I want you to help me understand what it means to you."

Michael, father of a fourteen-year-old boy, was very clear with his son about having parties at their house. "I know you kids use alcohol and drugs at parties, and I know you don't have the same values I have; but I don't want you having a party here with people using marijuana or alcohol. If I see anyone using them, I'll ask them to go home. If that will embarrass you, you need to work it out to have a party without drugs, or you can boot out your friends who are using before I boot them out. I know you feel differently about it, and I understand that. I know you think I'm old-fashioned, but that's how I plan to handle it in this house. I'm concerned and scared about the possible short- and long-range effects of teens using drugs, and, although I know I can't stop you from using, I prefer that it doesn't happen in our home."

Sometimes interventions have to be accompanied by hard choices on your part. When Thomas was eighteen years old, he was heavily into cocaine and marijuana. He went to a treatment center and did well for a while. Then he started using drugs again. His mother minimized the situation for a long time before she finally got the courage to tell Thomas that he could no longer live at home as long as he chose to abuse drugs. Thomas left, vowing never, ever to forgive his mother. One month later, Thomas wanted to come home and sleep on the couch for "just a few days" until he could find another place to live. Although Mom knew on one level that Thomas was conning and manipulating, she still found it very difficult to refuse such a reasonable request—for just a few days.

Addicts lie and manipulate, so it would be entirely predictable for Thomas to say things like, "Can I sleep on the couch tonight? I will be moving into an apartment real soon," or "I'm going to look for a job tomorrow," or "I can't believe you can just write me out of your life forever," and on and on.

Mom, remembering that Thomas was better at being the "look good guy" instead of the "do good guy," finally used an intervention when she said, "Thomas, I want to stop trying to control what you do, but I also plan to stop rescuing you when you get into trouble. I have faith in you to make decisions for yourself, to learn from your mistakes, and to figure out how to solve problems that come to you or that you create. Specifically, this means that I'll no longer provide a place for you to stay. It also means I won't badger you about getting back into a recovery program, but I will know when you are helping yourself. You know that I am always willing to help you when you are willing to help yourself."

Mom certainly found a way to get the message of love across without jumping in and rescuing her addicted son. In so many words, she was telling Thomas, "Be just the way you are; feel just the way you feel; do just what you think you want. I love you because you're you. I may not always like or agree with some of your decisions, and I'll probably let you know my thoughts and feelings, but it won't change my love for you."

Thomas knew his mother meant what she said this time. He lived on the streets for a week before calling his mother and letting her know he was willing to go into treatment. It takes a strong parent to make these choices. Too many parents fear their kids will live the rest of their lives on the street, so they continue to rescue. Most kids don't stay on the street. They find places to crash for a while, and soon, they are ready to come home again or get into treatment or therapy. It's the kids who are rescued over and over who end up with the most serious addiction problems or even end up committing suicide.

There is a lot of help out in the world for you if you are struggling with a teenager abusing drugs. Getting help means you are wise enough to make use of all the support that is available through friends, therapists, support groups such as Al-Anon, parenting books, drug-information books, and treatment programs that have intervention specialists.

We often explain to our clients who seek therapy that they are now in the league of champions who are wise enough to know they need a coach. Olympic champions or championship ball teams would not even consider trying to function without a good coach. The champions still have to do all the work, but the coach can stand back far enough to see with perspective and objectivity. The coach teaches the necessary skills, but the champion still has to practice to apply the skills. Just look for a coach who can help you fight drug abuse using prescription-drug-free methods—one who understands abuse and isn't trying to convince you that your teen has a mental illness.

Alcoholics Anonymous has some of the best suggestions for helping you keep the faith when dealing with an addicted son or daughter. You may have seen the bumper sticker that reads, "Let go and let God," or maybe you've heard the serenity prayer: "God grant me the serenity to accept the things I cannot change, the courage to change the things I can, and the wisdom to know the difference." Use these and other inspirational quotes to help you remember that most teenagers grow up. The teenage years are not forever. You were once a teen yourself, and you made it and so will your teen.

## TEEN SEXUAL ACTIVITY, PREGNANCY, AND SEXUALLY TRANSMITTED DISEASES (STDs)

As parents, you may want to think your teens are asexual, just waiting until they are older for you to give them the "big talk." Guess again. Your teen may have a very different value about sexual activity than you do. Many teens are not only sexually active at a very young age but also experience multiple partners. Sex games are becoming more prevalent at teen parties. Many teens think having oral sex is an activity and not "sex."

It is important to discuss your concerns about the spread of sexually transmitted diseases, as well as to share your values and be open to hearing your child's values. Never label your child or disrespect him or her by calling the teen names like "whore," "slut," or "pervert." Instead, be curious and ask your teens what their thoughts are about teen sex and let them know that you hope they won't engage in behaviors where they don't love and respect themselves.

It is not unusual for some young people to experiment with bisexuality and to question their sexual preferences. Because many young people feel embarrassed to talk openly with their parents about sex, you might find another place where your child feels safe to discuss concerns and issues.

The greatest contributor to teen pregnancy is the lack of sex education and a failure on the part of the significant adults in teens' lives to acknowledge and cope with teen sexual activity. You really can't avoid sex education, because even refusing to talk about sex is a form of sex education that could invite damaging conclusions such as "sex is secret, bad, and not to be discussed with your parents." In most cases, these conclusions don't prevent sexual experimentation. They just invite guilt, shame, and silence after it has already taken place. We suggest that both parents talk about sex with their children, discussing the difference between sex and love. Make discussion, not agreement, the goal of conversations on sex education.

Prevention of STDs is best accomplished by using condoms, and yet most teens are not likely to have the nerve, the money, or the desire to go to a store to buy them. Teens are certain they are invincible and may even think they are immune to STDs. For this reason, some parents have decided to keep a supply of condoms next to the extra soap, toothpaste, and toilet paper in the linen closet, even if they themselves feel uncomfortable talking with their kids about sex or their kids feel uncomfortable talking with them. Yet these parents notice the supply has to be replenished from time to time, and they feel it is the least they can do if their teens or some of their friends have decided to be sexually active.

Parents who buy condoms for their teens may or may not approve of their kids having sex, but they don't want to see their children get STDs or bring children into the world before their teen is ready to parent and love them. One out of four female teenagers will be pregnant before the age of twenty. Therefore, within the bounds of your religious, moral, and ethical beliefs, it is important that you develop a strategy for dealing with your adolescent's sexuality.

## SEXUAL ABUSE AND INCEST

Sexual abuse is one of the most painful dysfunctional systems for anyone to deal with. Emily, a thirteen-year-old survivor of incest, talked about her pain in a counseling session. She said, "My pain hurts so much inside of me, but no one wants to see it. Sometimes it hurts so much I want to die, but then I tell myself this isn't going to hurt forever. I cry myself to sleep and try to make the pain stop, but the scars are deep. I think I can't go on, but I know I must try. I want to believe that everything will get better, and I want to give hope to others who have the same pain as me. We have to believe that happiness is waiting for us." Emily's experience wasn't uncovered until her mother went to a therapist to deal with some other issues. Mom was feeling a lot of pressure in the family, but she couldn't put her finger on any one thing. She simply knew it just didn't feel right around her house anymore, so she decided to go in for counseling. As a result, she became more open and emotionally honest. Her improved communication skills started rubbing off on her thirteen-year-old daughter. One day, her daughter told her that one of her relatives was molesting her. It ultimately came out that there had been sexual abuse in this relative's home for years, and nobody had known. This is not unusual in a dysfunctional system. Because denial is such a big part of dysfunction, many people won't admit there is a problem until it slips out.

Emily's upbringing had been very strict, and her parents had overprotected her. Emily's family taught her to do as she was told and to listen to grown-ups. Because her siblings had been rebellious, Emily took the "good, compliant child" role in the family. She focused on doing what others wanted. In some ways, Emily's molestation was an extension of her thinking—she couldn't see an alternative to doing what older people wanted her to do. When the perpetrators asked her to cooperate, she worried that she wouldn't be loved if she said no. Luckily for Emily, when she told about the abuse, her mother never questioned the truth of her statements.

We cannot emphasize how important it is to take your kids seriously when they tell you something of this nature. They have already experienced a great deal of shame, guilt, and degradation. They have felt isolated and thought of themselves as "bad." The last thing they need is for you to question or blame them.

Once again, this is an area where outside help is essential through therapy or group support. Many communities have Parents United programs and other similar services to help you deal with sexual abuse and incest.

Most often, the perpetrator of incest or sexual abuse will deny that it happened and accuse the victim of lying. Their denial is similar to the addict who is protecting his use. In this case, the perpetrator may also be saving face. Nevertheless, he or she, too, needs help. Perpetrators' healings begin when they find out they are still worthwhile human beings with certain behaviors that must stop immediately. They need to hear that help is available to deal with the feelings, thoughts, and behaviors that brought them to this situation in the first place.

The healing process for someone who has been molested is a long one, but it is much easier if your child can be helped before he or she represses the information. Otherwise, it can take years and years of pain for the information to surface again so that it can be dealt with. Repression never makes the pain go away. Only talking about the problem and dealing with the feelings can do that.

Just as in chemical dependency, the healing process involves the entire family, as all of you have a reaction and are affected by the problem. Those family members who are unwilling to participate in therapy and self-help groups continue to suffer until they do get help.

## CUTTING

How do you know if your child is cutting? It's usually very difficult to know, as teens do a terrific job of hiding this behavior from the world. They cut in places they can cover, wearing long sleeves or long pants to hide the scars or raw cuts. They don't talk about what they are doing, and, usually, they hide this behavior even from their friends. Your best clue is to pay attention to whether or not your teens show arms or legs. Sometimes the best you can tell is that your teens aren't themselves or that their friends come to you with concerns. They may have seen some of the cuts or scars or are worried because your teen/their friend is not him- or herself. You can simply ask your teen, "Are you cutting yourself? I haven't seen your arms or legs in ages and I'd like to. You're not in trouble, but if you are cutting, we need to get some help as you must be feeling very discouraged."

A young girl who had been cutting offered to let us share the following essay in the hope that it might help others who are dealing with cutting. We couldn't say it better!

> *First of all, the worst thing a parent can do is tell the kid they have nothing to be upset or sad about. For one reason this is usually untrue; teenagers can have a lot of issues they choose not to share with their parents and having a parent tell a teen their life is easy and they have no problems just makes the teen not want to talk to the parent at all about what's bothering them and makes them feel like their parent doesn't care enough to be involved in their life. Another mistake a parent can make is asking if they're doing this because everyone else is doing it. That can be interpreted as an insult to the teen's character. Contrary to many adults' belief, we don't just jump off a bridge because other people are doing it, too. Cutting is a personal problem, not a peer pressure problem. And cutting is usually looked down upon in high school social circles anyways.*
>
> *I think it's good for parents to know the logistics of why teens cut and not every teen cuts for the same reasons. Some cut to get rid of the numbness. After a traumatic situation numbness is often something teens feel and it's not a fun feeling. To have no feelings isn't something people want and cutting is kind of a way to "snap out" of a numb state. It's a way to feel because they'd rather feel pain than feel nothing.*

Some cut because they think they deserve it; it's their own form of punishment because of how much they hate themselves. Generally when teens cut they are in a sort of dissociative state. They don't feel the pain as they normally would. And parents shouldn't confuse self-harm with liking pain because it's not the pain they like, it's inflicting it upon themselves. I've heard cutting described before as being locked in a room with the person you absolutely despise followed with the question, wouldn't you want to hurt them too? Some parents really don't understand the concept of self-harm and I think it's important they do. Your kid isn't crazy, they're just a person who needs help and you need to treat them like a person, not a basket-case.

Also, I believe chronic cutting is a lot more serious than a one-time incident. If a teen does it once and decides it's a bad idea and stops that's a lot more normal. I know of some people who have tried and they have no underlying issues and are pretty healthy overall. A onetime incident needs to be addressed differently than multiple ones. Usually if a teen cuts many different times there is an underlying problem. Getting the teen a therapist can be helpful, or getting them to talk to their parents or a close sibling or role model. But you can't force a cutter to talk about it. They are most likely going to be unwilling to talk and hesitant to let anyone help them. Being there for the teen is the most important thing. Let them know you're there for them and you will love them no matter what. But give them their space. Being smothered isn't going to help anything. Getting clean from cutting is an independent thing. A cutter won't stop just because someone tells them to; they need to go through a process to realize cutting is not the solution and it's a process they have to do themselves. For a cutter to stop, they have to want to stop.

One last thing is if a teen is cutting, it's usually not the only form of self-harm they've tried. Burning, purging, and starving themselves are a few common ones. So these would be issues that need to be addressed as well. Teens also need to know that these are serious issues and can cause long-term effects, such as cutting too deep and losing *a lot of blood can cause serious blood problems that affect their life as an adult.*

Though this young lady didn't mention it, sometimes kids cut because they don't like how they are feeling and in an effort to get control over their feelings, they cut, because the feeling that results from that is completely in their control. Kids have said, "I'd rather feel the pain I create than the feelings my friends and family have inflicted upon me."

## TEEN SUICIDE

Losing a child is the most difficult experience parents could ever face, and losing a child to suicide may be doubly hard. We wish we could give a formula to make sure no one ever has to go through this kind of pain, but that isn't possible. All we can say is that it's vital to heed warning signs and get help immediately.

Suicide is a choice that is too often made from a place of deep discouragement. When your teens lose self-confidence, suicide becomes one of their choices. A loss of self-confidence coupled with the belief that control is out of their hands may lead to teen suicide. Many teen suicides are also drug related. If your kids haven't been learning how to cope with life's difficulties themselves, or how to solve their problems and stand on their own feet, suicide may look like the only choice left to them. Many kids haven't learned that making a mistake is just an opportunity to try again, and not the end of the world. Unfortunately, because teens can be so intense and dramatic, they may choose a "permanent solution to a temporary problem."

Find opportunities to discuss that last statement with your children even before they become teens. Ask them what they think it means that suicide is a *permanent solution to a temporary problem.* Ask them what other solutions a discouraged person could choose. If kids have a chance to think about other possibilities before suicide becomes a possibility, they are more likely to know how to seek help until this time of discouragement passes.

The following list of warning signs came from http://www.teensuicide .us/articles2.html: disinterest in favorite extracurricular activities; problems at work and losing interest in a job; substance abuse, including alcohol and drug (illegal and legal drugs) use; behavioral problems; withdrawing from family and friends; sleep changes; changes in eating habits; begins to neglect hygiene and other matters of personal appearance; hard time concentrating and paying attention; declining grades in school; loss of interest in schoolwork; risk-taking behaviors; complains more frequently of boredom; does not respond as before to encouragement.

Take your teens seriously if they exhibit signs of suicide. Encourage them to talk to you or help them find someone they can talk to. Show concern and really listen, even if they have threatened suicide in the past without following through with action. They need a ray of hope to let them know that, however bad it may seem now, there is a tomorrow when "this too shall pass."

One mother who suspected her daughter might be thinking of suicide told her, "Honey, I remember a couple of times when I felt like committing suicide. I felt so bad; I couldn't imagine things getting any better. But they did. I hate to think of how much I would have missed if I had killed myself. For one thing, I would have missed you."

When talking to your child about suicide, it's important to use words such as "suicide" and "death." Don't shy away from these terms for fear of introducing an idea that you think your teen doesn't already have. Ask if they have a plan or if they've tried already. Finding out their plan shows you how far along they are in their thinking—a teen with a plan is like a loose cannon.

You can ask your child how his life would be different if he killed himself. By doing so, you'll probably find out what is really troubling him. Don't hesitate to seek professional help if there are any indications of suicide.

Stella felt helpless to deal with her daughter Traci's discouragement. Traci was acting more and more unhappy. Stella asked Traci if she would see a therapist. Traci agreed but wanted her mother to go with her. The therapist asked Traci to fill out a different kind of "pie" chart than the one described under sibling rivalry in Chapter 12. This chart listed four slices of life: family, friends, school, and love. Traci was asked to rate each slice of the pie from 1 to 10, with a 10 representing the best. Traci marked a 2 in family slice (her parents were talking divorce, but she loved both parents very much), a 0 in the friend slice (she had just had a huge fight with her best friend and thought there was no hope of a resolution), a 1 in the school slice (she was failing—probably because of all the other problems), and a 10 in the love slice (she felt the only good thing in her life was her supportive boyfriend).

The counselor said, "No wonder you are feeling so discouraged. Three out of four areas of your life seem very dismal. However, did you know that suicide is a permanent solution to a temporary problem?"

Traci thought about that, and then asked, "Do you really think these other problems are temporary?"

The counselor asked, "What do you think?"

Traci said, "I guess they are, but I don't see any solutions now."

The counselor asked, "Would you like some help with solutions?"

Traci said yes, and the counselor suggested they tackle one at a time. Traci chose the friend slice. The counselor role-played with her on ways to talk with her friend to solve their problem. Traci left feeling very encouraged and hopeful. She said, "I know things will get better. I certainly wouldn't want to try a permanent solution to a temporary problem." That statement had obviously made a deep impact.

## EATING DISORDERS

When some scary behaviors such as sexual activity, suicide, or sexual abuse are involved, you may have a tendency to ignore the topic and hope it will take care of itself. But when diet is concerned, you, like most parents, probably take the opposite approach and become overly involved in an area that is often none of your business.

Parents' concern for the health of their children can get out of proportion around the subject of food, especially because many of you have your own hang-ups about weight, looks, and diet. You try to be good parents by making sure your kids eat properly. Quite often, instead of providing healthy choices and trusting your kids to eat when they are hungry and stop when they are not, you interfere in this natural process and, without knowing it, plant the seeds for eating disorders.

The media might have a strong influence on trends today. Teens see skinny rock stars and dancers (not realizing how much exercise they get from so much dancing and practicing), and photos of teen models (not realizing how these photos have been through airbrushing and other Photoshop techniques). Have a discussion with your teens about what they are seeing in the media and magazines. Use curiosity questions to invite them to think about what it takes to be like that and what ideas they have to accept themselves as they are.

Most eating disorders start in childhood. For many different reasons, some children stop regulating their eating internally, stop listening to their bodies' cues, and no longer trust themselves to eat what is right for them. Because everything can be intense and extreme when kids are teens, problem eating in the younger years can take on serious and even life-threatening proportions in the teen years. One teenager was a picky eater when she was younger. However, when she entered high school and experienced teasing about being overweight, her pickiness became more extreme. She started eating very little and then discovered how good it felt to throw up and get rid of what she did eat. She became bulimic.

In the most extreme cases like the above, teens completely stop listening to their bodies' cues to the point of near death.

Some of the most common eating disorders we see in teens are extreme obesity; anorexia, or near starvation by a restricted amount of food intake; and bulimia, a condition in which people binge on food and then induce vomiting or use laxatives as a means to stay thin. The last two patterns are found mostly, but not exclusively, in females.

Just like chemically dependent people, teens experiencing eating disorders come to a point where they can't stop their damaging behavior without help. Their eating patterns are no longer voluntary but compulsive.

If your kids' eating disorders have moved into the extreme, get professional help, which includes a trip to the doctor to check out your teen's physical condition, a series of appointments with a therapist, and help from a dietician if needed. In an extreme case, your teen may first need to be stabilized medically before he or she can learn to change the symptoms and deal with the deeper issues in therapy. Once again, the greater the involvement of the family in the therapy process, the faster the healing for the teen.

## YOUNG ADULTS WHO WON'T OR CAN'T LEAVE HOME

Today we have a new phenomenon—kids who won't leave home. These are people in their twenties who have still not become responsible adults with good judgment.

In view of the problems we've been exploring, it may be surprising to think of children who won't leave home as exhibiting dysfunctional behavior; but we think children who lack the courage or the drive to start their own lives away from their families have serious problems. We are also concerned about the changes in our culture that leave many parents thinking it is their job to provide room and board, advice, cars, money, and maid service to their young adults. There was a time when mothers dreaded the day of the empty nest, when their children had all left home and left them feeling no longer needed. Today, many parents long for an empty nest, wondering if their grown children will ever leave home and be on their own.

Why are thousands of adult children still living at home with their parents? Many kids want to live at home because they can't live anywhere else in the style to which their parents helped them become accustomed with so little effort of their own. Other kids stay home because their overprotective parents have completely convinced them that they'll never make it on their own and there's no point in trying. They've lost faith in themselves. Some stay home because they have an alcoholic or severely discouraged parent who they are convinced will die without them.

Some kids stay home because they can't find jobs and they can't afford to live outside the home. If your kids are working hard at finding work and contributing with help while they live with you, that might be a good temporary solution. If they are acting like they are looking for a free ride, that's a problem. Even when jobs are tough to find, kids can live communally with their friends, sharing rent and rooms and couches. They can also look for work with nonprofits that offer free room and board in exchange for free labor. Sometimes that can be a stepping-stone to something better in the future.

If your adult kids are living at home, the kindest thing that you can do is move them out eventually. You can give them a deadline and offer to help them find a job, make a budget, or find a place to live. If you would have helped a child financially who went to college, consider helping the non-college-bound young adult with a small monthly stipend until he or she gets started. The best rule of thumb is to help those who are helping themselves.

## SUMMARY

We'd like to offer you a ray of hope. Even when times are tough, there are lessons to be learned and opportunities for growth. You can always control your attitude, even if you can't control behaviors or external factors. By adopting an attitude that nothing is forever and that there is a silver lining, who knows, you might even come out of the scary times feeling grateful that you and your kids learned, grew, and became more resilient from the experience.

## KIND AND FIRM PARENTING TOOLS TO REMEMBER

1. When your teens do something that scares you, tell them that it scares you. Ask them to stop doing the scary behavior, letting them know that what they are doing may not be a problem for them but that the thought of losing them is a problem for you. If they understand your reasons, they just might comply, especially if they respect your opinion.

2. Don't expect your kids to deal with gangs, bullies, and violence alone. Find ways to help them through whatever difficulties they encounter.

3. Remind yourself about the continuum of drug use if you start panicking. Review the different parent behaviors for each stop on the continuum.

4. No matter how worried you are about the right way to say things, let go of your fears of making a mistake and make an effort to talk with your teen, to say what you think and feel. Not talking is worse.

5. If an intervention is in order, give it a try. You'll get many chances to try again even if the first, second, or third ones don't work.

6. Most teens today are sexual beings whether you approve or not, so start talking with your teen and creating a dialogue rather than trying to get promises that probably won't be kept.

7. If you think that sexual or physical abuse is occurring in your house, get help quickly. You won't be judged; you and the rest of your family will get a release from the pain.

8. Take all threats of suicide seriously enough to talk with your teen either by yourself or with the help of a counselor. Even if your teen uses the expression, "I could kill myself," as a way of making a point and not as a threat, you need to explain why that particular comment isn't helpful and suggest some other ways to express feelings.

9. Stop trying to control what your teens eat or how they look, and watch many eating disorders disappear as if by magic.

*Practical Application Activity*

### Teen Secrets

It's easy to "catastrophize" the outcome of normal teenage behavior and to believe that how your teens are now is how they will be forever. Remembering your teen years can relieve your worries and restore your faith in your teens.

1. List at least three things you did as a teenager that you didn't want your parents to know about.
2. Are there any entries on your list that you still have never told anyone?
3. What relationship, if any, do you see between your own teen secrets and your fears or judgments about your teen?
4. Your teens love it when you share some of your secrets with them so they don't feel like they're the only "bad" people in the family. It makes you seem more human, too, which is a real asset at this time.

# 14

## ARE YOUR UNRESOLVED TEEN ISSUES GETTING IN YOUR WAY?

### REPARENTING YOURSELF

Raising a teenager brings up a lot of unresolved issues from your own adolescence. Anything that didn't get worked out when you were a teen still lurks in the shadows of your unconscious, waiting for another chance. Even though these issues are below the surface, they influence how you parent your teen. Not only does the old baggage you carry around with you from your teen years get in the way of living a full, rich life; it often creates stumbling blocks when dealing with your teen.

Going through your teen's adolescence gives you another chance to work through some of these issues. In doing so, you will experience countless benefits. You'll be a more effective parent, have more compassion, understand your teen better, and heal the teen within you.

If you think about the issues your teens are dealing with, you won't be far from identifying the unresolved issues you still need to work out for yourself: power, self-image, body image, intimate relationships, friendships, relationships with your parents, and independence.

Here's a quick activity to help you get in touch with some of your unresolved issues. Think about where you lived and went to school when you were between the ages of thirteen and eighteen. Now answer yes or no to the following questions:

Did you believe in yourself and know you could make your life work (power)?

Did you feel good about yourself and think you belonged (self-image)?

Did you feel comfortable in your own body (body image)?

Did you have a boyfriend? Girlfriend? Did you date? Were you comfortable with people of the opposite sex? Same sex (intimate relationships)?

Did you have friends that you hung out with and enjoyed spending time with (friendships)?

Did you trust your parents and feel you could go to them when you needed adult guidance and wisdom (parents)?

Did you have freedom in your choices or were your activities determined and monitored by the adults around you (independence)?

When Morgan took the survey, she discovered that she had unresolved issues about self-image, body image, and intimate relationships. She thought about how this was impacting her relationship with her teens and realized that she was terrified they would suffer the pain she did as a teen. To make up for her lack of confidence in those matters, she gave her kids free rein when it came to having boyfriends and girlfriends, let them pick out their own clothes and "look," and ignored her daughter's frequent diets to maintain her slim figure. If her kids wanted a piercing or tattoo or wore makeup, she breathed a sigh of relief that they knew how to fit in without her help.

After answering the questions about her own teen years, she was wise enough to know that she couldn't help her kids with things she hadn't worked out herself, but she could have conversations with her kids about those areas by being curious and concerned. She could ask her friends or siblings to mentor the kids in these areas so that they had a "wise" adult if they needed help.

Morgan also spent a lot of time working on her own issues while her teens were individuating. She began studying nutrition, got involved in jogging and yoga, and started asking her friends to help her update her "look." Modeling self-care can be a powerful tool for your teens.

Leo also answered the questions and learned about his unresolved issues. Leo grew up with a single working mom who gave the kids a lot of freedom. They were very self-motivated, because no one was there to manage or motivate them.

Occasionally he and his sister would spend a night at his dad's place. His dad was very strict and repeatedly told the kids they could be anything they wanted to be but it was up to them to make it happen. Leo thought he could not seek help from either parent. He believed his father was too busy, and he didn't want to make demands on his mom, who was working and running the household by herself.

Even though Leo became very independent, he felt neglected. Now he overindulges his two kids because he wants to be a hands-on parent, involved in their lives. He's a bit surprised that the kids don't take any responsibility around the house and expect him to drive them everywhere and arrange their busy schedules. Leo is torn. On the one hand, he would like his kids to be less spoiled, but on the other hand, he really wants to give them what he didn't have as a kid.

Another mother shared a problem with her sixteen-year-old son, Cody. His economics teacher called to say Cody had been tardy or absent six days out of ten. The teacher wanted to know what Mom was going to do. Without a second thought, Mom said she would come in for a parent-teacher conference.

When asked why she responded that way, Mom said she wanted to look good to the teacher. Upon further exploration, she realized she was automatically intimidated upon hearing the teacher's voice and immediately thought she had done something wrong. Immobilized, she turned her power over to the teacher.

Mom realized, with help from her parenting group, that she held a childhood belief that to be worthy of love or friendships, she could never be wrong. When she thought she'd made a mistake, she immediately tried to fix the situation to the teacher's satisfaction. So intent on doing what was "right" in the eyes of others, she couldn't see what was "right" for her son—and herself. In this case, she was more focused on staying out of trouble with the teacher than in helping her son.

If Mom hadn't been so caught up in her unresolved issues, rather than accepting what the teacher said at face value, she might have talked to her son to find out what he felt was going on and what he wanted to do about it. She could have asked the teacher if he had discussed the problem with her son. Mom could also let the teacher know that although she didn't approve of her son's behavior, she thought it was up to him to work it out with the teacher. She could ask her son if he wanted her to go to school with him to discuss the situation with the teacher or if he would like to handle it on his own.

Knowing your areas of strengths and weaknesses from your teen years will help you avoid letting those old insecurities influence how you parent your teens. You can use the information that follows to help you resolve old issues so you can be an empowering, encouraging, and effective parent of your teens.

## BEING ON YOUR OWN SIDE USUALLY HELPS YOUR TEENS

If someone asked you, "Are you on your teenager's side?," the odds are good that you would say, "Of course I am!" (even if your actions might indicate otherwise). But are you on your own side? You might think you are even though you may be like most parents who don't realize they have a right to a life separate from their children and that parents don't have to dedicate every action to their teens.

Being on your own side means you consider your needs as much as you consider those of your teens. When your fears become the basis of your thoughts and actions, then actions become the dance of the "mischief shuffle," a dance that ignores self-respect and self-care. Mischief is doing anything that doesn't meet the needs of the situation and isn't respectful.

## THE MISCHIEF SHUFFLE

The mischief shuffle (a relationship dance, not to be confused with a collection of songs on an iPod) consists of the mischief you create with thoughts and actions that get in the way of your long-term parenting goals and your self-respect. This shuffle not only keeps you from being on your teen's side, but also keeps you from taking care of yourself with dignity and respect. Some of the most common characteristics of this dance help you justify short-term parenting techniques (such as control or permissiveness).

### MISCHIEF SHUFFLE STEPS THAT KEEP YOU FROM BEING ON YOUR OWN SIDE

1. Trying to fix everything that goes wrong, rather than allowing teens to grow by fixing their mistakes. This attitude also distracts you from fixing your mistakes while you busy yourself rescuing your teen; to be on your side you need to learn from your mistakes and teach your kids that they can learn from theirs.
2. Worrying about what others might think, which makes looking

good more important than finding out what is best for your teens and for yourself. You cannot be on your own side when you are busy trying to please others who aren't really involved.

3. Trying to protect teens from all pain, which also protects them from learning and growing into capable adults. Being on your own side means facing some of your own pain, forgiving yourself, and allowing yourself to grow.

4. Being afraid of your teen's anger, which means giving up, giving in, or doing whatever it takes to avoid the wrath of your teen. This teaches teenagers that anger is bad and should be avoided or that it can be used to manipulate others. Instead, show that anger is a valid feeling and can be handled appropriately. Being on your own side will make your teens angry at times, especially when you say no when you believe it's right for you.

5. Believing that you are selfish if you aren't self-sacrificing, which means you're never allowed to enjoy yourself. Being on your own side means finding your own balance between doing things for yourself and doing things for or with your children.

Being on your own side means understanding your own individuality, just as you understand the individuality of your teenagers, and supporting your own growth with dignity and respect, just as you support your teen's growth with dignity and respect. Your teens will give you many opportunities to work on taking care of yourself.

If you feel stuck in your old issues, we recommend reviewing this chapter often. Try the activity at the end of the chapter to help identify your unresolved teen issues and put them to rest. What you learn from the experience will enrich both your life and your teen's.

## KIND AND FIRM PARENTING TOOLS TO REMEMBER

1. Look at having a teenager as a wonderful opportunity to get rid of old baggage from your teen years, instead of dragging it along with you or dumping it on your kids.

2. If you have issues about your self-image, your teen is sure to bring them to the surface. It's time to separate your issues from your teen's issues.

3. Paying attention to your fears can be an excellent way to zero in on past problems. As you understand what your fears are, you can let them go and deal with the real needs of the situation, not just those you imagine.

4. With new perspective, options appear, as if by magic.

5. Remember back to your own teen years to look for parallels between your memories and your current situation with your teen.

6. Don't forget that the pain of most losses you experience is short-lived and that your teen will constantly be moving in and out of your life.

### Practical Application Activity

Use the following activity to identify unresolved issues from your teenage years and to put you in touch with your teen's world. Instead of thinking like a parent "should" think, you will be able to recall how you thought, felt, and behaved when you were a teen. You will begin to remember what it was like to be a teenager, which gives you a better understanding of your teen's perceptions and shows that you may be taking some of your teen's behavior much too personally.

## DISCOVERING YOUR UNRESOLVED TEEN ISSUES

1. Think of a situation that occurs with you and your teen that you wish were different. Describe the specifics of the situation in writing.

2. How do you feel when the situation occurs? Be sure to use feeling words and not words such as "that," "as if," or "like." A feeling can be described with one word. If you use more than one word, you are describing what you think. For example, "I felt as if my teenager hated me" is a thought. "I felt hurt," on the other hand, describes feelings. (You can be experiencing more than one feeling

and can use as many single words as it takes to describe them, but they won't be in complete sentences: mad, sad, helpless, and so forth.)

3. What is it that you are doing in the problem situation?
4. What is your teen's response to your behavior?
5. What is your decision about your teen's response?

## REMEMBER A TIME FROM YOUR OWN TEEN YEARS

1. Think of a time when you were a teen and things weren't working out the way you wanted them to. Describe the specifics of the situation in writing.
2. How did you feel about the situation?
3. How did you behave in the situation?
4. How did the adults around you or your parents behave in the situation?
5. What was your response to their behavior?
6. What did you decide about the situation?

## USE INSIGHTS FROM YOUR PAST TO HELP YOUR PRESENT

1. Review what you wrote about the previous two situations. Describe an issue that remains unresolved from your own teenage years.
2. What information, if any, did you get from your teen memory that can help you deal more effectively with your current problem situation?
3. If you're having trouble figuring out the connections, share your answers with a spouse or friend who can be more objective about you. Perhaps they can see solutions and patterns that are too difficult for you to see yourself.

# CONCLUSION

## FROM FEARFUL PARENTING TO COURAGEOUS PARENTING

I t wasn't too long ago that the word "teenager" could not be found in the dictionary. In those days, adolescents served an apprenticeship to learn a skill, got married, and often did not live past the age of thirty-six.

Although political, economic, technical, and health standards have changed dramatically in our society, it seems to be more difficult to catch up with emotional and social changes. Parenting skills have definitely not improved. Today there is a focus on making children happy and helping them develop healthy self-esteem. Yet parents still use the old methods of overcontrol or overprotection, which makes it difficult for children to feel good about themselves. They develop an "entitlement" mentality—expecting their parents to make them happy.

The emphasis on homework and grades has created tremendous stress, power struggles, and rebellion. It can be very confusing to teens when their parents seem concerned about their happiness and self-esteem but spend so much time badgering them about grades and trying to control their every move—either through punishment or bribes and rewards.

Your challenge as a parent is to grow and change as fast as the times, and as fast as your teenagers. Change isn't easy, but of course you can do it—if you know it is worth it. The first step is to stop treating your children like babies, especially your teens. You need to treat them like people who are worthy of respect and who are capable of learning, contributing, and growing.

It can be very difficult to let go and believe in the basic capability of your teenagers to learn without being controlled or overprotected by you. A basic reason for this difficulty is not understanding the difference between fearful parenting and courageous parenting.

*Fearful Parenting*

Fearful parenting is not letting go because it is too hard. You may feel scared and fear permanent damage if you let go. You may think control works. Another form of fearful parenting happens when you don't see small-step alternatives to control, so you think your only choice is to do nothing, and that isn't okay with you. You may think control or permissiveness is the only option.

Fearful parenting is worrying more about what others might think or say than doing what is best for your teenagers, including allowing them to learn from their mistakes. It means being more interested in perfection than in the growth of your teenagers. You think it's your job to "overparent." Maybe you don't have anything better to do. Fearful parenting is reactive because you are sure that you have only one chance to deal with any given situation and you don't dare make a mistake or your child will suffer irreparable damage. Fearful parents don't mean to hurt their children, but there are many things they do unknowingly that stunt their teens' growth and development. Overprotection, control, rigid rules, permissiveness, and a lack of communication are but a few of the methods that contribute to stealing strength and capability from teens.

### Courageous Parenting

Courageous parenting means facing the fear (yes, it is scary to let go and allow your teens to make mistakes) and doing what needs to be done anyway. Courageous parenting means taking the time to teach skills even though it's easier to criticize or rescue. Courageous parents have faith in their children to learn from their mistakes in a supportive atmosphere that does not include criticism or rescuing. Courageous parenting is having faith in the basic capabilities of your teenagers and knowing they can learn when given the room and support they need.

When you think of your teens as competent and capable people who have the ability to learn what is good for them through experience, it's easier to be courageous.

### Accidental Empowerment

Sometimes teens are allowed to work things out for themselves simply because their parents don't know what their teens are doing so they don't interfere. Roy shared an example of accidental empowerment:

> *I'm so glad I didn't know Ian was cutting classes to go surfing for most of the school year. He had a friend in the attendance office who was covering for him, and his grades were A's and B's, so I never found out. When Ian finally told me about his escapades, I said, "How could I have missed all that?" He said, "Aren't you glad you did? We would have been fighting constantly and it wouldn't have changed anything except our relationship. I learned what I needed to learn, too, when I couldn't get into the university because of my grades and had to start off in the state college. But you know what, Dad, I'd probably do the same thing all over again. I've made tons of great friends both surfing and at the college, and it cost a lot less for me to figure out what I wanted to major in."*

If you are a courageous parent, you need to:

1. Surround yourself with other people who have the same goals. (This may mean starting your own parenting support group or working with a therapist who understands and promotes Positive Discipline.)
2. Practice kind and firm parenting skills.
3. Teach skills to teens so they can manage their own lives.
4. Read this book again and again. You will learn something new with every reading.

Parenting teens is an art form and it requires a big commitment on your part. You need to take time for training yourself, as many of the Positive Discipline parenting methods don't come naturally. The great news is that the more you practice respectful relationships with your kids, the better your skills and theirs will be in all relationships.

# ACKNOWLEDGMENTS

Thanks to our kids and clients and workshop participants who have helped us learn the lessons of parenting teens—over and over again.

Thanks to our editor, Nathan Roberson, who was extremely helpful and supportive of our many requests.

Thanks to our husbands Hal Penny and Barry Nelsen, who are endlessly supportive and pick up so many pieces when we are knee-deep in a book deadline.

# INDEX

# ABOUT THE AUTHORS

JANE NELSEN is the author and coauthor of twenty books and is a licensed family therapist with a doctorate in educational psychology from the University of San Francisco. She finds much of her material as the mother of seven children, twenty-two grandchildren, and two great grandchildren—and a very supportive husband. She wrote the first Positive Discipline book in 1981. Later she teamed up with Lynn Lott to write *Positive Discipline for Teenagers, Positive Discipline A–Z, Positive Discipline in the Classroom, Positive Discipline for Parenting in Recovery,* and *When Your Dog Is Like Family* (an ebook). Many books in the Positive Discipline series have followed, and now have a following of thousands in many languages.

LYNN LOTT is the author and coauthor of eighteen books and is a licensed family therapist with a master's degree in marriage and family counseling from the University of San Francisco (1978) and a master's degree in psychology from Sonoma State University (1977). She has been in private practice since 1978 helping parents, couples, teens, and individuals and now does therapy with clients all over the world through Skype. In her spare time, Lynn is an avid skier, reader, cook, and hiker. She resides in California and Florida with her husband, Hal Penny. Lynn is the mother of two, stepmother of two, and grandmother of six. For more information about Lynn, visit www.lynnlott.com.

Together, Lynn and Jane have created training workshops in *Teaching Parenting the Positive Discipline Way* and *Positive Discipline in the Classroom.* Dates and locations for these live workshops (and the DVD training formats for people unable to travel to live workshops) can be found at www.positivediscipline.com, where information also can be found about parenting classes taught by Certified Positive Discipline Parent Educators in the United States and other countries.